LUCKY

LUCKY

ED JACKSON

ONE PLACE. MANY STORIES

HQ
An imprint of HarperCollins*Publishers* Ltd
1 London Bridge Street
London SE1 9GF

www.harpercollins.co.uk

HarperCollins*Publishers*
1st Floor, Watermarque Building, Ringsend Road
Dublin 4, Ireland

This edition 2021

2
First published in Great Britain by
HQ, an imprint of HarperCollins*Publishers* Ltd 2021

HB ISBN: 978-0-00-842336-0
TPB ISBN: 978-0-00-842337-7

MIX
Paper from
responsible sources
FSC
www.fsc.org   FSC™ C007454

This book is produced from independently certified FSC™ paper
to ensure responsible forest management.

For more information visit: www.harpercollins.co.uk/green

This book is set in 11.7/16 pt. Sabon

Printed and Bound in the UK using 100% Renewable Electricity at
CPI Group (UK) Ltd

In loving memory of my late friend, Tom Maynard. For giving me the strength to carry on.

'You have power over your mind – not outside events. Realise this, and you will find strength.'

—MARCUS AURELIUS

CHAPTER 1

NO DIVING

There's a number; there has always been a number. As long as I can remember, this number has followed me everywhere. Not in a creepy, stalkerish way; more like a guardian angel. I had played number eight throughout my professional rugby career, and I had met my fiancée, Lois, on 8 January. I'm sure you have your own number, the one you would call 'lucky'.

So, looking back, it came as no surprise to me that 8 April 2017 was the first scorching hot day of the year. Following a long dreary winter, this was the day I'd been waiting for. After bundling my dad and stepmum into the car, I drove over to their friends' house. After lunch, I headed down the winding stone staircase to the pool; I was excited by the thought of cooling off and spending a good hour floating on a lilo.

Life had been pretty good recently and I felt that everything was slotting into place. I had just signed another two-year contract with my rugby team, the Dragons, and Lois and I were preparing for our summer wedding in the Tuscan countryside the following year.

I kicked off my shoes and unbuttoned my shirt. Humming to myself, I imagined the swimming pool at the Italian villa where we would marry, filled with all of our friends.

I walked to the edge of the pool and dived in.

Immediately, a shockwave rolled through my body; I had hit my head on the tiles at the bottom of the pool. Everything went black.

There was a loud ringing in my ears as my vision returned. I glanced around; I was still at the bottom of the pool. After ten years in professional rugby, I'd had my fair share of knocks, but this . . . I'd never hit my head like this before.

I tried to stand and check if I had cut myself. Nothing responded. I tried again. Nothing. My arms and legs hung limply at my sides. The only thing I could do was move my head. I was completely immobile, face down, at the bottom of the pool. Confused, I told my body to push me up again but it no longer responded to my requests. My heart began to hammer in my chest as confusion gave way to panic.

My body went into overdrive, pumping adrenaline to allow me to enter fight or flight mode. But I couldn't do either. The adrenaline that was supposed to help save me had nowhere to go. Instead, it threatened to tip me into terror.

All my senses were heightened. With my mouth firmly clamped shut, my eyes darted left and right as I searched for something to help me. My chest became tighter. I needed air. I hadn't taken a big enough breath before diving in. Even though I only had the use of my eyes, I wanted desperately to fight for my life. If no one had seen me dive in, then only I could save myself, I thought.

The seconds ticked by as I stared at the tiles on the bottom of the pool.

Try again. You've got to try again.

I strained to push myself up, but all that happened was a precious air bubble escaped from my mouth. I began to feel light-headed and I squeezed my eyes shut, trying to think. Shit.

And then, it wasn't just me. The water pushed at my body, threatening to roll me but also letting me know I wasn't alone. Strong hands gripped my arm, pulling me up, turning me. My face broke free of the water and I gasped for air, over and over again.

I opened my eyes to see my dad standing beside me in the pool. His gaze darted over my body as he began to check me over. A retired GP, having worked his way from a council estate in Sheffield to Oxford University, he was the epitome of the unflappable Yorkshireman.

I stared down at my body. My right leg was hanging down and I thought I could feel the ridges of the tiles against my heel; my left leg had decided to float near the surface.

I was still dazed from the impact and grateful that Dad had taken control of the situation. I reassured myself that after a couple of minutes the feeling would come back. Then we could all laugh about the time I made a clumsy dive into the shallow end of a pool. A welcome feeling of calm washed over me.

Dad checked me over with one hand, while the other one supported my head. My friend, Daffyd, was on the other side, supporting my torso with both arms. Together they floated me over to the edge of the pool and my head came to rest in the hands of Diane, a family friend, who was waiting for me by the side of the pool.

As another friend called for an ambulance, my elation at having been pulled from the bottom of the pool began to ebb away. Staring down at my lifeless body bobbing in the water, I realised that I wouldn't be hauling myself out of the pool, wobbling over to a sun lounger and laughing about my lack of diving prowess. There wouldn't be a hastily made sign propped up next to the pool saying, 'No Diving . . . Ed'. This wasn't going to turn out that way.

Dad had made the decision that I shouldn't be lifted out of the pool until the ambulance came. I tried to distract myself by letting my eyes roam over the endless blue sky. There was no pain; in fact, I couldn't really feel anything at all. Peering down at my legs, I noticed that my right leg had floated up to join my left. They looked like they were still attached to my body, but they certainly didn't feel like it. All I could feel were Diane's hands cradling my head and the water lapping against my shoulders.

The minutes ticked by slowly as we all retained our positions, frozen to the spot. As I listened to Diane's reassuring voice, I began to feel sleepy in the warm sunlight. Maybe I could just nod off for a few minutes? I would wake up when the ambulance arrived . . .

'How about your left hand?' Dad's voice cut through my thoughts, keeping me present. 'Can you move that?'

I tried. I really tried to move my left hand.

'Anything?' I asked.

'What about your right hand?'

He hadn't answered my question. Instead, he squeezed his eyes shut – just for a moment – but I had caught the flash of panic in them. This was more than a bump to the head.

All I could do was try to stay calm. There was nothing I could do to help.

Eight months earlier . . .

After a half-day drive up the Pacific Coast Highway, Lois and I had pulled over and found the trail that led into Pfeiffer

Big Sur State Park. Through the trees the path wound, the redwood trunks shooting up to the sky but still allowing the dappled light through. There was no one else around and we both felt as if this woodland was just for us. A couple of miles into our journey, the path fizzled out and we were left with two options, to turn back or to push on and make our own trail.

Granted, getting eaten by a black bear probably wasn't high on TripAdvisor's list of 'Things To Do In California' but the allure of a bit of adventure was always too tempting. We went with option two.

Three hours later, we were still in the forest, clambering over fallen redwoods and wading through mountain streams. The hike was starting to take its toll.

I studied the map for a few minutes before rotating it ninety degrees. Lois caught me and raised an eyebrow. 'Don't worry, Lois. It's fine, I know where we are.'

She didn't believe me and neither did I.

Just as I was wondering whether we'd become the next warning story the rangers would tell other tourists, we emerged from the tree line. Up ahead was the most breathtaking view of the Pacific Ocean. There was nothing but Lois, myself and the endless sea crashing against the cliffs beneath us. We stopped to rest and gave ourselves time to absorb the moment.

During the long nights in hospital that were to come, when my mind started to wander, I often escaped to that place. I would close my eyes and take myself straight back. I drew comfort from the warmth of the sun on my face, the smell of the salt in the air and the shades of blue where the sky met the Pacific.

To think we could have taken the easy option, given up and turned back. To think we would have missed that moment because we were afraid of a little adventure. Life is an adventure and sometimes the path disappears; push on and make your own path.

It's strange how your mind can try to shield you from the reality of a situation or flip you full force into worst-case scenarios.

On that hot April day, in the ambulance to Royal United Hospital in Bath, my thoughts were racing. Every eventuality was going through my head, but when my mind wandered towards the negative, I would distract myself by skipping to a positive outcome. This is what helped me the most in those first few hours. Denial or not, it was keeping me calm and if you're calm then you're still in control.

As we sped along the roads, sirens blaring, that calmness turned to tiredness and I wanted to close my eyes.

'You have to try and stay awake, Ed,' the paramedic said, watching me closely.

I stared up at him. He was being unreasonable. I needed to sleep; surely there was no harm in that?

'Ed, stay awake now. Don't go dropping off.'

Knowing that the hospital was only a fifteen-minute drive away, I begrudgingly agreed to try to stay awake for him.

What I didn't know at the time was that my mind was protecting me from a reality that was very different. I found out a year later that my fifteen-minute journey had actually taken two and a half hours. Three times the ambulance had pulled over for me to be resuscitated. There had been a doctor in the back of the ambulance shooting me full of adrenaline, just to keep me alive. My heart had stopped beating three times. Technically, I had died.

My life didn't flash in front of me. I didn't see a light or hear a guiding voice. Instead, I floated in and out of reality. I had been given a glimpse of how easy that final step can be. It's just like going to sleep. You drift away, unaware that you might be closing your eyes for the final time. At that moment I was grateful that I had been shielded from the reality of my situation, but soon I would have to face it.

A shaft of electric light projected across the ceiling of the ambulance as it pulled up at the hospital doors. My gaze was fixed firmly upwards, the two foam blocks on either side of my head not allowing even a millimetre of movement.

Still lying flat on the trolley, a strap across my forehead to keep my head from moving, I emerged from the back of the ambulance and into the evening warmth. The light had started to fade, and, as I was wheeled under the hospital porch, I looked up at the large backlit sign that read 'Accident and Emergency'.

I had visited this hospital sporadically since I was born, due to mishaps as an adventurous child and various rugby injuries, but this time the word 'Emergency' wouldn't leave me. We rolled over the threshold and entered the unmistakable fluorescent lights of the hospital corridor. My vision sharpened as the incandescent light flooded the space around me.

The light was overwhelming. Unable to turn my head to the side, I closed my eyes. My focus settled on the rhythm of the wheels rolling over the floor beneath me. Every bump or crack resonated through the trolley and my panic increased. Movement had become my enemy.

At the sudden halt of the trolley, I blinked my eyes back

open. I had come to a stop in a bay. Voices circled around me, my dad's amongst them. There was a sense of urgency in the conversations at the end of my bed. Occasionally, out of the corner of my eye, I caught sight of a shoulder, hand, or the back of someone's head.

Five minutes passed. Everyone was talking about me, but no one was talking to me. Lying in the hospital bed, I felt incredibly vulnerable.

Finally, a flash of blonde hair came into view, and I recognised my fiancée, Lois. Before I could speak, she faded from view as the medical staff in their blue and grey scrubs carried on with their work. I strained to find her again, but she was gone.

My chest tightened. 'Lois?'

A voice came from behind the figures. 'I'm here, Ed. They'll let me through in a minute.'

I didn't know what to say to reassure her, to smooth away that note of panic in her voice. What do you say to people in this situation? I couldn't tell her that I was fine, because clearly that wasn't true . . .

The sea of scrubs parted and in a second Lois was by my side. She leant over me, trying to smile, her bright, brown eyes full of concern.

'Don't worry,' I said. 'I think the pool's okay. I didn't crack any of the tiles.'

She reached for my hand. I couldn't feel her touch.

'Don't worry about it,' she said, her smile not quite able to reach her eyes. 'I'll send the pool a "Get Well Soon" card. I'm sure it's just bruised.'

Seeing Lois's face made everything more real. My mood suddenly dropped and an overwhelming feeling of guilt washed over me.

'I'm sorry.'

A cold shiver passed through me as the heavy fog of shock began to wear off. I was left with only the stark reality of my situation. I could tell from the activity going on around me, and the fact that I still couldn't move or feel anything, that this was serious.

Silent tears streamed down my face. This was the woman who had chosen to spend her life with me. Was she now tied to a very different man? Lois didn't deserve this. She was young, athletic, full of irresistible energy and plans for our future together. And I couldn't even fulfil the simple act of taking her hand in mine.

Before she could respond, Lois was ushered away so the nurses could prepare me for an MRI scan. I barely heard them speak, my mind preoccupied with the worst-case scenarios that had now come into play.

Will I play rugby again? Who will look after me? Lois? My mum? It's not fair on them; they don't deserve this, I'll be a burden that they'll grow to resent . . .

I pushed back at the negative thoughts and tried once more to distract myself. I started to count the ceiling tiles as we made our way down a long corridor, anything to keep my mind occupied. The fear would come in waves: one moment I would be happily asking the porter if he'd had a busy night; the next, my chest would tighten and a bubble of panic would choke me, cutting me off mid-sentence. I kept on trying to distract myself from the reality of the situation, anything to keep my mind occupied and diverted.

The results of the scan were not good. I needed an immediate operation, and so, an hour later, I was being transferred to Southmead Hospital in Bristol. I had been told it was the best place for me as it had a leading neurological department. It was certainly different to the hospital in Bath; it had a multi-million-pound intensive care ward that was the newest in the country. I tried to take it all in as I was wheeled through the entranceway. Up above was a huge glass ceiling. It was dark by now, so there was no chance of seeing the outside world. Reflected back at me was the distant figure of a lone man lying on a hospital bed, being pushed through a hospital vestibule.

The on-call neurosurgeon, Mr Barua, was ready for my arrival even though it was getting very late. Mr Barua was a smartly dressed man, particularly for two in the morning. It was Mr Barua who told me that I had dislocated my C6 and C7 vertebrae, which are at the bottom of the neck. The disc in between the two vertebrae had exploded and splintered shards of bone had lodged in my spinal cord.

The spinal cord is usually 12mm across and, judging by the scans, I was told that I only had about 4mm left. I was literally clinging on by a thread. Those remaining nerve fibres also didn't mean I would be able to walk again, despite my initial hopes that I would. My prognosis was uncertain and first I had to have an operation.

Mr Barua came closer as he explained that he wanted to create an incision in my throat to perform surgery on my spine. He would then insert a cage around my spine and remove the shattered disc.

I'd had six previous operations due to rugby injuries, so I was familiar with the possible risks of a general anaesthetic. But the way Mr Barua relayed them to me was new – he meant it when he told me that I might not wake up again.

As I lay in my hospital bed, all I could do was stare up at the tiled ceiling. Even if I wanted to look away I couldn't: my neck was still braced and a white chest plate had been added that made me look a bit like a Stormtrooper. All of this was designed to prevent any movement of my spine.

I had been in the same position for five days. The only way I could change my view was by closing my eyes. These were my options – stark white ceiling, or the back of my eyelids.

The first few days after the operation were a bit of a blur. A constant stream of nurses, doctors, friends and family rotated around my bedside as I tried to put on a brave face and take everything in. They were all welcome distractions.

At least I no longer had a drain and tube running down my nose and throat. Coming around from the operation on my second day in hospital with those in place had been terrifying. Multiple wires and tubes had snaked out of my body and I couldn't remember why I was in there. Worse was to come. I hadn't been able to cough after I had lost the power in my chest and abdomen. This meant that every time fluid had lodged in my throat, I had started choking. The panic of not being able to breathe again had taken me straight back to the pool. Straight back to drowning.

Friends had popped in and out during visiting hours. They had been wide-eyed the first time they registered all of the wires and beeping machines surrounding me, trying to mask their shocked expressions. This kept on happening. People would walk into my room and their faces would betray them; the colour would drain. I couldn't see myself, couldn't see the tubes, so I used their reactions to try to monitor my situation. It soon became a scene I would have to play out, over and over again. A friend would enter with a fixed smile, which would slowly slide away, shock would take over, and I would spend the next hour reassuring them that I was still me.

My rugby friends were different. They instinctively knew that normality was needed. My former teammate, Si, decided to cheer me up by buying me a present. On his first visit he chucked three juggling balls at my bed. I watched, unable to move, as they bounced off my chest onto the floor. 'There you go, pal. Seeing as you're going to be here for a while, you might as well learn a new skill.' Some people would think this was insensitive; I thought it was hilarious. And I needed to laugh.

These welcome visitors had brought with them gifts of food and were eager to distract me from the static hours lying in a hospital bed. I was being fed through a tube, so I couldn't sample any of their edible offerings, but I was happy to watch them tuck in – room 11b had turned into an all-you-can-eat buffet.

I was only allowed two visitors at a time. Lois and my old school friend, Tom Souto, had been keeping me company on the morning of my fifth day in hospital. Everything in my room was new. The white fittings were scuff-free and the grey laminate floor looked unblemished by the patients who had come before me. I was still getting used to living on the set of an American hospital drama – it was so different to the ramshackle wards I'd been in before. They had used as much glass as they could wedge in and it was clinical to the point that I didn't want us to make a mess of their shiny new intensive care department. Every evening, my mum would circle the room and tidy up, so that we could reset for the next day.

'You're doing great,' Souto said for the third time. He was picking his way through a giant hamper at the end of my bed. With a grunt of approval, he pulled out a bag of salt and vinegar crisps. 'Do you mind if . . . ?'

'Course not, it's not like I can eat them,' I said over the

beeping machines that surrounded me. I still hadn't got used to them and found them distracting, especially when they sped up or slowed down.

'You're much better than two days ago,' Souto said, between mouthfuls of crisps. 'Doing really great.'

The sharp tang of vinegar hit the air and my stomach rumbled. At least I hadn't lost my sense of smell.

'Thanks, mate.'

'It's the truth, you really are.'

Mum popped her head around the door to tell us Mr Barua was on his way and she was going to find my dad. That day was the day we'd been focusing on for the past seventy-two hours. I'd been instructed to wiggle, clench and stretch for the last five days. Below my neck, everything remained still, apart from some slight movement in my right arm.

Souto said his goodbyes. Through the glass wall of my room, I could see him greeting another of our friends, Jack, who had come to visit. The door hadn't quite closed behind him and their voices drifted through to me.

'How's he doing?' Jack asked Souto.

'Oh God, he's absolutely fucked!'

Lois glanced over at me and I rolled my eyes. 'I can still hear you, Souto!'

There was silence. Souto popped his head around the door. 'You're doing great, Ed. You've got this.'

I grinned at him. 'If you say so.'

Unless you know someone who has been through a similar situation, you are rarely prepared for the curveball you've been thrown when the unexpected happens. You are at a sudden low point, probably mentally or physically at your weakest, and then you are supposed to make some of the most important decisions of your life.

The first challenge when these curveballs happen is therefore finding the one thing that will steer you through these unfamiliar waters. My paddle came in the form of knowledge; if I knew what I was facing, then I was better armed to deal with it.

Early on in my hospital stay, my younger brother, Josh, helped me immeasurably with this when he came into my room one day carrying an iPad.

'I know I don't have much to update you on,' I teased, 'but I don't think my conversation is so poor that you'll have to watch films during your visit.'

'Ah, but that's where you're wrong,' Josh responded, as he started clipping the iPad to the extendable arm that hovered over my bed. 'This isn't for me, it's for you.'

'So, you'll put the film on for me?'

He gave me a look that told me that I didn't understand much. 'No, you can put it on yourself using only your voice.'

And he was right. Within an hour I was able to do nearly everything someone with a working finger could do.

In the quiet of the evenings when I didn't want to be lying in silence, I would research my situation using voice-activated commands. These are some of the bits I found out in the first few days:

- It's estimated that 50,000 people in the UK are living with a spinal cord injury. This meant I had a fair few co-conspirators to track down.
- Each year, approximately 2,500 people in the UK are newly injured. That's about a 1 in 27,000 risk of suffering a spinal cord injury.

- The most common causes of spinal injuries are falls, road traffic accidents and sport. Diving into the shallow end of a swimming pool, because the ripples from a water feature make you think the water is deeper than it is, falls into 'unclassified trauma'. (A couple of years later, I met a man in a spinal unit I was visiting. He told me that he'd been left paraplegic when the bus he'd been on had fallen into a ravine after a bridge collapsed. 'Now that's a proper way to get a spinal injury,' I thought.)
- The higher up on your body your spinal cord injury is, the more movement you will lose.
- People with spinal cord injuries to their back have para-plegia. This affects the movement and sensation in their legs. People with spinal cord injuries to their necks are quadriplegic. Quadriplegia affects the movement and sensation in both your legs and arms – a '2 for 1' in the neurological condition's aisle.

As I read about these injuries late at night, the glow of the screen my only company through the long night-time hours, I slowly came to realise that I wasn't alone. Learning about my injury helped me understand that however bad I thought my situation was, there were thousands of people the same or worse off.

Mr Barua was a busy man, but one to whom I owed my life – for seven hours he had picked parts of my exploded disc from my spinal cord using a magnifying glass. So, I didn't mind that I'd had to wait for him as he checked on his other patients.

A couple of medical students trailed in after him, always

two steps behind. They stood in the farthest corner, there to observe rather than assist.

'Ed, how are you feeling today?' Mr Barua asked, after he had inspected the chart at the bottom of my bed.

'Stronger . . . I think.'

'Good. I'm glad to hear it.'

He circled around the bed and Lois pushed her chair back so he could stand next to my head, where I could get the best view of him. It was touches like this that made me like him.

All eyes in the room were trained on him. No one spoke, as if they were encouraging him to fill the silence.

'So, we have compiled the results of the American Spinal Injury assessments.'

I blinked, unable to nod encouragingly. This is what I'd been waiting for, the outcome of this mess. Would I ever be able to move again? Would I ever be able to walk again? And, most importantly, would I ever be independent again?

'I am sorry to say that you are ASIA Category A.'

I had no idea what he meant, but from his tone I could tell that this was not the outcome we had been hoping for.

'What about the bit of movement I've got in my right arm?'

'I'm sorry, but that doesn't change our findings.'

'What am I looking at then?'

'It's likely that you won't be able to walk again.'

'So . . . paralysed?' I asked. I felt that this was important enough to need complete clarity.

Mr Barua nodded.

Mum burst into tears.

'And best case?'

'We're hoping you get the use of your arms back so you can use a wheelchair.'

Lois was crying now too.

'If there's hope for me regaining the use of my arms then . . . maybe, one day . . . my legs?'

'Ed, I'm very sorry, but that's not likely to happen here. The tests show no sensory and almost no motor function below the site of your injury. With this type of quadriplegia, regaining the use of your arms would be considered an excellent recovery.' He looked around at the rest of my family before his gaze settled back on me. He wanted everyone to be on the same page. 'It's unlikely you will ever walk again. You need to come to terms with that.'

No one wanted to be the first to speak.

'I'll be back again tomorrow,' Mr Barua said, nodding at his two students to follow him. 'And, Ed, I really am very sorry.'

That evening, after the visitors had left, I gave myself time to digest what the doctors were trying to tell me. I had to set the tone of this thing, because these injuries hadn't just happened to me; they had happened to everyone who cared for me as well.

I allowed myself to reflect for a moment. How could this have happened to me on 8 April of all days? It was supposed to have been a good day; it had always been a good day. So much for my lucky number . . .

It's unlikely you'll ever walk again. You need to come to terms with that. That phrase kept circling around my mind.

'Bollocks to that,' I concluded. If there was still even a tiny chance of me being able to walk again then I was going to take it.

With sudden clarity, I realised that if 8 April had not been a good day, it had been a lucky one instead.

The bottom line was that the day I'd dived into the pool I got lucky. I got lucky that people were there to pull me above the water. I got lucky that my dad is a doctor and knew to keep my spine straight. I got lucky that I was only ten miles from one of the leading neurological centres in the country. I got lucky that I was operated on within seven hours of the injury.

I was lucky to be awake and talking. Now I was lucky there was a chance that I would regain the movement in my arms. I had asked myself whether I was a lucky or unlucky kind of person. The answer was that it was entirely up to me – it was just the way I looked at it.

Luck had got me this far, but I was still paralysed and immobile on a hospital bed.

My journey had only just begun.

CHAPTER 2

THE FINGER

'How about now?' I asked, opening my eyes.

'Nope, nothing happening here, bud,' said Murph, my friend from Cardiff, as he peered at my big toe. 'Try giving me the finger again.'

I closed my eyes to allow myself to really concentrate, really focusing on firing the signals to my right middle finger. It was my sixth day in hospital, and nothing had changed. No movement from the neck down, apart from my right arm, despite practising all day.

The news that I was unlikely to walk again had spurred me on. Having lost the movement in my right side last, I was concentrating most of my efforts on my right big toe and right index and middle fingers. I'd been told that if movement was going to come back, it would start with the side that last had it. My right arm was becoming stronger, but there was still no movement in my hand. Heck, sometimes I tried to move my whole left leg, just to mix it up a bit, but only when I was feeling particularly ambitious.

I shot another message down to my middle finger. The problem with doing this was that, with my eyes closed, my mind would trick me. I would send the signal and I'd feel a twitch. We'd quickly learnt that it was better that I waited for the opinion of an independent adjudicator.

'Nothing, bud,' Murph said. 'Why don't I scratch your foot again?'

This was something that Murph excelled at. If someone ran their fingernail along the base of my right foot, my whole leg would spasm. I loved it. It was the only time my legs would move. Murph, good friend that he was, would spend hours running his nail up the base of my foot as I grinned at the automated reaction of my leg jerking upwards. It wasn't a real movement, I knew it didn't count, but it felt like something was still working down there.

One of the nurses came into the room. 'I have a ten-minute break, so I thought I'd come and see how you're doing.'

'Look,' I said, as Murph ran his finger up my foot again. 'It's aliiiive . . .'

She smiled and made a mock jump, before taking a seat. We all chatted for ten minutes. I enjoyed having the company of three people in the room as the hospital's two-person rule was wearing a bit thin. It meant that, if a couple came to visit, Lois would have to leave and sit outside, even though she wanted to see them as much as I did.

Throughout the day, a rotation of friends and family came in to check on me, update me on the outside world, steal my food and keep my spirits up. Not that I needed any buoying; I felt it was my duty to be upbeat. It wasn't all about me; this accident had affected every single one of them. All day long, as these visitors trotted in and out, I would send the signals to my body to move, hoping that one would reach its target.

That word, 'independence', stalked me every hour of the

day. I wanted to regain a degree of independence so that neither Lois or my mum would have to spend the rest of their lives caring for me. If in six months' time I hadn't made any progress, I could live with that if I knew I'd given it everything. But what I couldn't live with was knowing that I'd only given it half a go – I wouldn't be able to look either Lois or my mum in the eye.

So, I spent every second I could firing those signals and making jokes. By acting positively for other people, I was also starting to feel positive.

The last of my visitors had left. I strained to hear their voices fade away down the corridor, before the ward door slammed behind them, sharply cutting them off.

It was 8 p.m. and the next twelve hours stretched in front of me. Every day, time slowed at that point. It no longer clipped along at a steady pace; instead, it had some fun with me. 'So, you thought that was thirty minutes?' Time asked. 'You lose again; it was closer to seven.'

I stared around my overwhelmingly empty room. The helium balloons in the corner didn't seem to sit right anymore and jarred my line of vision. I nudged my eyes towards the door, unable to move my braced neck even a millimetre to the side. The chest plate always felt heavier at this time of night.

Intensive care units are not like other hospital wards. When I'd previously stayed overnight in hospital for one of my various rugby injuries, I'd been monitored but also encouraged to rest. Lights had been switched off at what was deemed bedtime and my carers retreated to the nurses' station at the end of the ward. Intensive care has one sole purpose: to keep you alive.

Everything else fits around that single commandment – and rightfully so.

At night, the door to my room was always wide open and the medical staff would regularly pass by, talking amongst themselves. At all hours, patients would be rushed past my doorway, flat out on a hospital bed, sometimes a team of doctors doing everything they could to save a life. This was never a place of silence.

As I stared at the door, one of the machines in the room next to me sounded out. Alarms blared along the corridor and I frowned at the noise. Something wasn't right. Within seconds, two nurses ran past my room, followed by a couple of doctors a few minutes later. I rolled my eyes up to the ceiling and hoped that my neighbour would make it.

I had to distract myself. I asked my iPad, which was hanging over my bed in front of my eye-line, to play a film. I hoped I'd lose myself in it for a couple of hours. If this didn't work, I could always record my diary.

I've always found having distractions is one of life's most important hacks. As a kid, it was easy; everything was a distraction. I would finish school and become a dinosaur for an hour, and suddenly all the stresses of being a 7-year-old were a thing of the past. Then as I got older, and schoolwork became more significant, it was sport that became my sanctuary.

But, without realising it, by my early twenties I had become completely consumed by sport. Yes, I had other interests, such as video games or nights out, but neither of these was particularly fulfilling or required my entire focus. For me, distractions only work if they have a productive outcome, as well as passing the time.

Therefore, in my mid-twenties, I decided to start a distance learning degree in Business Leadership and Management, which was a great distraction from sport. It calmed the emotional extremes of my daily life. No matter how badly I'd played at the weekend or how long my shoulder injury was taking to heal, I had another interest to take my mind off rugby. And that's the kind of distraction I needed now.

It had all gone quiet further down the hospital corridor. Was this a good or bad outcome? I didn't want to ask; the medical staff had more important things to deal with. Maybe someone would let me know tomorrow. I tried to concentrate on my film. A gun-toting man was driving a truck the wrong way down a freeway. Cars spun out of its way, crashing into barriers.

Will Lois leave me if I stay like this? No one would blame her if she does . . .

I pinched my eyes closed and tried to get back to my film. It was no good; the thoughts about my future swirled inside my head, and even the film's gunfire and bomb blasts were doing little to divert me away from them. Why hadn't anything moved yet? I was no medic, but I knew the longer there was no movement, the less likely there would be any. I'd read about spinal shock, where there is a loss of movement because the body shuts down to protect the spinal cord. But that only lasts for five or six days. This was my sixth night in hospital; I was past that point now.

I shot another signal down to my finger and stared at it. Staccato clips of a turf war getting out of control exploded on to my screen. I tried to time the signal to my finger with the ammunition rounds being shot. Nothing. None of my friends and family had said it, but they must have thought it – days had passed, and still no movement. Trapped in my spiralling thoughts, it was time to pull out my best distraction.

Pausing the film, I opened the notes on my iPad and began recording the second entry in my diary via voice command.

'It's been six days since my accident and I've got to say that I didn't expect the evenings to last so long . . .'

It was comforting to hear the words aloud. I'd never kept a diary before, so I'd been amazed on my fifth night in hospital that speaking out loud about my day, transferring these thoughts out of my mind, gave me some peace. They were no longer trapped inside of me, unable to find an outlet or conclusion. They were pushed away, and I was left able to rest. Before this discovery, I couldn't turn my brain off, so I'd been unable to fall asleep.

When I'd finished my entry, the fizzing in my head subsided. I felt very much in the present, not missing the past or worrying about the future – it was time to sleep.

There is not much of a bedtime routine for a quadriplegic in intensive care; I didn't even have my teeth brushed as I had difficulty swallowing. So, I turned my iPad off and closed my eyes.

BeepBeepBeepBeep.

My eyes flicked open and I gasped in a lungful of air.

It had happened again. The machine that monitored my heart rate had thought I was going into cardiac arrest.

A nurse popped her head around the door. 'Everything okay in here?'

'I'm not dying, don't worry. Are you sure there's no way you can change it?'

'Sorry, Ed, but we can't override the settings. We would if we could.'

I tried to push down the anger I felt at rarely being able to sleep for more than a few minutes. Every time I fell asleep, my heart rate would dip under 40 beats per minute (bpm), which is alarming for a machine that is monitoring your blood pressure. It thinks you are about to die. Most people's heart rates range between 60 and 100bpm when they fall asleep. But, as I was a trained athlete, years of intensive cardio had meant that mine dipped below 40bpm, which set the machine off constantly throughout the night.

I tried to look at it in a different way. Rather than feeling angry at my heartbeat dipping below 40bpm, I instead tried to be grateful that at the time of the accident I was physically fit. I might not have survived otherwise.

'At least I got forty minutes that time.'

I closed my eyes.

The clatter of heavy footsteps woke me. I blinked and scrunched my eyes at the harshness of the electric lights. I tried to lift myself off the bed.

Why can't I move? Am I still asleep? Where am I?

'Sorry to wake you, but it's time for your checks,' one of the nurses said.

With a rush, everything that had happened in the last week came back to me. One of the cruellest things was that, just for a moment, I had been back to normal and now I had to process what had happened all over again.

On each side of me were two nurses and the fifth one stabilised my head and neck. It had to be midnight as my last check had been at ten and they happened every two hours. That meant I'd had thirty minutes sleep – my blood pressure hadn't dipped below 40bpm yet.

'One, two, three.'

I tried to make myself as light as possible, although I knew there was nothing I could do to help them. As I weighed eighteen stone, it took five of them to safely roll me on to my side. They began to inspect my shoulder blades, bum, thighs, calves and heels for the first signs of pressure sores. These are the creeping enemy of anyone who has to lie in the same position all day. If the nurses didn't check for them and treat them quickly, layers of tissue could die and have to be surgically removed. With that in mind and however annoying it was, I was happy for them to inspect away.

When they were finished, the nurses returned me to my back but angled me slightly on to my left, so the pressure was taken off the right side of my body for the next two hours. This pleased me as this direction was away from the door, which meant the light from the corridor was slightly fainter and there was a better chance I might get some sleep – you had to take the small wins when you could. I tried to focus on this as I willed myself to relax.

'All done, we'll see you at two.'

I tried to get back to sleep but my neck ached and my thoughts had started up again.

When I was 23, one of my best friends, Tom, died. There had been three of us – Tom, Rich and me – best friends since the first day of secondary school and into adulthood. Whatever we went through – exam panics, dating dramas, the slow climb of growing from boy to man – we were there for each other. And then Tom died, and there was only two of us left.

I had been in Croatia with Lois and my family when it had happened. Every year we went on holiday to the same remote fishing village and, by the third day of our trip, we had completely relaxed in the familiar seaside setting.

The call from Tom's sister had come through when I had been getting ready for dinner. Lois had found me sitting in the shower, fully clothed, completely unaware that my nose was bleeding from the stress the news had already placed on my body.

The following months were the toughest of my life. Losing a friend who was just at the start of his life, the unfairness of it all, plagued me. I could have stopped living, hid myself away, let grief take me. But whenever I thought of taking that route, I would imagine what Tom would have said about it: 'Feeling sorry for yourself isn't going to change anything, you've still got a life to lead.' So I learnt ways to cope. I had to, as I knew I wouldn't come out intact if I didn't. At my lowest moments I always thought of Tom, nothing would be as bad as when he was taken away from us. I had survived that; it had even made me stronger. And so I knew I would survive this too.

I closed my eyes again.

I was drowning.

I couldn't breathe. I was back in the pool.

My eyes flicked open.

It's okay, you're not in the pool, you're in hospital.

I breathed in but the air wouldn't go all the way in; something was blocking it. The drowning sensation stayed with me. I needed to cough, clear the mucus that had built up and gone down the wrong way. I couldn't turn on to my side. I hadn't even got the strength in my chest to cough. So the phlegm just sat there, blocking my airway. I needed the cough machine to clear my lungs and I needed a nurse to fit it.

I made a gurgling sound, trying to call for help. I couldn't press the buzzer, for obvious reasons, so I made the gurgling noise again. My eyes darted over to the door. I was choking now, and my panic rose. Come on . . . come on . . .

Footsteps were coming down the corridor and I hoped that they didn't turn off into one of the other rooms. I made the loudest noise I could, which was a mixture of a strangled frog and the air being released from a balloon.

The footsteps quickened and in a few seconds the nurse had pushed a suction tube down my throat to clear the first lot of phlegm. She then pulled the cough machine's mask over my face. I stared up at her as the machine pumped two lots of air into my lungs and then sharply sucked the mucus out of me. It was an odd sensation and it may have sounded disgusting – but don't be rude about my new best friend. Me and cough machine were inseparable.

It's overwhelming to think about what a simple thing like coughing means to your body. Willing myself to fall asleep, I tried to think about how amazing the human body is, but my mind kept on drifting back to the fact that I couldn't even cough.

I took myself back in time to the Pacific Coast Highway. Lois and I had pushed our way through the forest; it had smelled of moss after the rain had cleared some of the heat. I'd known that in a moment, tired but happy, that we would burst out onto the cliff face overlooking the sea.

I closed my eyes.

Alarm . . . Roll . . . Alarm. Drowning . . . Alarm . . . Roll.

'Morning,' Lois said, as she bounded into my room. 'How was your night?'

Bloody hell, it was good to see Lois.

Mum and Lois were keeping me company on my seventh afternoon in intensive care.

My mum is supermum. She will out-mum even the best of them. She lived the farthest from the hospital, yet she would be the first to arrive, and last to leave. She would also bring half the contents of the M&S food hall with her, even though I couldn't eat anything. When she couldn't be in the room with me, she would try to tempt the medical staff with a spare smoked ham sandwich or mozzarella pasta bowl. Mum dealt with my accident by being constantly by my side, while still trying to care for everyone else within a fifteen-metre radius of me. I loved her for it.

Mum was sitting on the chair to my right, nearest the door, and Lois was on my left. They were talking about Lois's upcoming netball tour and I was only half listening as I shot messages down my limbs, trying to get something to work.

I took a sharp breath. There was a twitch; I'd felt my right index finger twitch. It was the smallest of movements and I thought I must have imagined it. I was so tired from lack of proper sleep that sometimes my vision blurred and rippled at the edges. I did it again – it definitely twitched.

'Mum, look at my finger. Look, look!'

I closed my eyes and sent the command.

The squeals from both my mum and Lois confirmed what I was hoping for.

'Try your middle finger,' Lois said.

I gave it a go.

'Never mind, darling,' Mum said. 'It will happen soon.'

I gave it another go.

Lois squealed.

I stared at my finger in disbelief. I wiggled them both at the same time and off they went, doing exactly what I told them to do. If I'd been able to, I would have hopped off the bed and done a victory lap.

Lois and Mum leant in to hug me at the same time. I took a deep breath in. This morning, I had no working fingers and now I had two. The tears silently spilled down my cheeks as I broke out into a wide grin.

CHAPTER 3

WIGGLING

Eight days earlier . . .

I ran my gaze over the lunchtime spread. It was the first hot day of the year, the one I'd been waiting for, and I'd been invited over to our family friends, Laura and Philip's house for the afternoon.

'Well, I think that's everything,' Laura said, as she popped a bowl of chutney and another of mayonnaise onto the long outdoor table. 'Help yourselves!'

I didn't need to be asked twice. I put down the signed Fleetwood Mac vinyl, *Rumours*, which Philip had been showing me, and moved over to the table.

I love my food and, to keep my weight at eighteen stone, I had to eat around four to five thousand calories a day. The one catch was that they had to be good calories, not eleven bags of crisps, a Dominos and a side of chicken wings. Although these did occasionally make the menu.

'So, your dad tells me you've been signed with the Dragons again,' Diane said, as she passed me a plate of baked salmon.

'I've got another two-year contract. It's a great bunch of lads, and it means I won't have to move again for a while.'

Lois and I loved our life in Wales. I'm as English sounding as they come, so it had taken a few weeks for the Welsh boys to warm to me and not go quiet when I entered the changing room. But I'd got there in the end after they saw that I worked hard and took training seriously.

'I've been in Wales for two years now,' I added, as I tore off a piece of baguette, still warm from the oven. 'In a year I'll qualify for residency. I could even play for Wales, if they'd have me!'

'Do you know the Welsh National Anthem, then?'

I leant over and speared my fork into another jacket potato. 'I'd say so. Although any Welsh person might disagree. My teammates say I massacre it.' I grinned. 'I belt it out anyway just to annoy them.'

My stepmum leant over. 'Ed and Lois have also got the wedding coming up next summer.'

'In Tuscany, isn't it?' Diane asked, sipping her water.

I nodded. 'Yes, in July. We've been together seven years now; it's just taken us a while to get around to organising it.'

'And that hasn't been easy to do, has it, Ed?' my stepmum said, leaning back in her chair.

'Things run at a different pace over there. The Italians have a word, *domani*, which means tomorrow. Whenever we call the suppliers to check how things are going, it's always "*Domani, domani.*" We have a secret weapon now, though.'

'What's that?' Diane asked.

'I have a friend who plays rugby for Palma and he's married to an Italian lady. She's started calling them for us. And "*domani*" doesn't really fly with Marina. You wouldn't mess with her.'

They both laughed before the conversation naturally turned to Diane's recent trip to Florence.

I looked up at the sun and took a moment to feel its warmth. I'm an outdoors person. No matter what the weather is, you'll find me outside. I can't stand being cooped up – I'm a free-range chicken. I stretched out my legs and felt a twinge in my calf muscle. After sitting at the table for close to an hour, I was beginning to feel restless. I glanced over to the stone steps that traced their way down to the other section of the garden. I knew they led to Laura and Philip's swimming pool and I was eager to try it out.

'This has been great, thank you very much,' I said to Laura, while patting my belly in appreciation. 'I think it's time for a swim . . .'

It was Easter weekend, eight days after my accident, and I was waiting for the last hour of the early morning to tick by before my visitors would arrive. I'd had a bed bath and a suppository, which is pretty much as spruced-up as I could get in intensive care. I knew that when Mum arrived, she'd pop some bunny ears on my head and my morning's preparations would be complete.

My spirits had been lifted by my wiggling fingers and the opportunity to suck on a bit of chocolate – my first solid food since the lunchtime meal I'd eaten before the accident. Yesterday, I had proudly shown my new doctor the two twitching fingers and he'd been genuinely pleased for me, but it hadn't changed his prognosis. It was still very unlikely that I would walk again – a finger was not a toe.

My family had spent the afternoon celebrating anyway, me along with them. We had cracked open our Easter eggs early, and they had talked about how far I had come and how I would be up and about in no time. I had smiled along with them, caught up in their enthusiasm. We'd all moved on to focusing on my big toe now. And that poor little guy, marooned at the far end of my body, was not responding as expected. Not a tremor or a twitch.

During the long night, I had thought about what my doctor had said and the situation had begun to sink in. I understood the potential implications of my injury, even if I refused to accept them. Staying positive was essential. However, the expectations of my family and friends weren't quite matching up with what the doctors were saying. I understood that doctors are inherently cautious; it's their job to ensure their patients understand what they are facing. I also knew that my family was going to be overly optimistic and I needed that optimism to help keep me in a positive frame of mind. But the optimism had turned on me – it had begun to feel like pressure. There was now an expectation that I would make a full recovery, and quickly. I felt that if I didn't do this, then I would be letting them all down. I would throw them back to what they were facing a week ago.

At 3 a.m. I'd had a revelation. I had to concentrate on short-term goals rather than long-term outcomes. I had to be happy that I could wiggle my finger, not sad that my legs didn't move. I'd still keep the faith that I would make further progress, but I wouldn't beat myself up if it didn't happen every day. All I could do was try.

One of my favourite nurses popped her head around the door. 'We have a plan. Are you in?'

I grinned at her. 'Whatever it is, I'm in.'

'Good, I'll be back in ten minutes.'

I couldn't decide what she was up to, but I could have a good guess. Being one of the few patients in intensive care who wasn't in a coma, I had got to know the medical staff better than most. For three days, I'd been badgering them to wheel me out of my room. I'd been in a sterile box for eight days and it was safe to say that it was driving me mad. I'd counted all the ceiling tiles (184) and knew at exactly what time of day the sunlight would hit my window and when it would depart. I had to get out of here.

In ten minutes the nurse was back with another of her colleagues. With an efficiency that would impress even Florence Nightingale, they began attaching monitors and drips on to the side bars of my bed. In under five minutes we were ready, and they began to push my bed towards the door.

The wheels of the bed squeaked in protest, as if they knew we were making an illicit journey. Tapping my right index finger along to the happy tune in my head, we rolled out of my room and down the corridor.

All of the machines attached to my bed beeped away, unperturbed by the change of scenery. We squeaked our way out of the intensive care ward and my smile grew bigger with every one of the nurses' steps.

Down the corridor we sailed, a confident Armada of three. People scattered out of our way and pressed their backs up against the corridor walls to allow us to pass. No one would dare cross in front of us; mine was a tank of a bed, big enough to support all the equipment needed to keep someone alive.

We stopped in front of a set of double doors.

'We have to get through the cardiology ward,' my favourite nurse said, who I had recently upgraded to favourite person (apart from Lois, of course). There was a note of worry in her voice; I imagine that what they were doing wasn't exactly permitted.

'What does that mean?' I asked, unsure of her instructions.

She leant closer. 'Look straight ahead. And don't make eye contact with anyone.'

My eyes widened for a split second, before I took control and positioned them firmly upwards.

'We need to get through without any questions being asked,' she continued.

I held my breath as I stared at the doors to freedom.

If you happened to be passing through the foyer of Southmead Hospital on that Easter weekend, you may have seen a strange sight. In amongst the families seated at the scattered tables and chairs of Costa Coffee was a magisterial intensive care bed. And on this bed, happily slurping away at a Salted Caramel Crunch Coffee Frostino through a long straw, was an immobile, neck-braced, rugby player. Whose hospital gown may have ridden up a bit too far to be decent.

My favourite nurse leant over and positioned the straw near my mouth again. I'm usually a black Americano kind of man, but I thought that this occasion called for a more decadent drink. I took a big slurp, enjoying the sights of the foyer. Life was carrying on, just as it had done before.

I was happy to be out having a coffee with friends, not sad that my legs didn't move.

That evening, back in my room, I thought about my trip out for coffee. It had given me the strength to consider a future where I wouldn't recover the use of my legs or even both of my arms. Life would still go on, whether I decided to take part in it or not. I knew that if I was going to stay this way, then I was going to have to find a way of adjusting to it.

Through rugby, I already knew about a couple of people

who'd had spinal injuries before my accident. The first was Matt Hampson who, when he was 20, had a scrum collapse on him, dislocating his neck. He sustained a spinal cord injury at C4/C5, which is two vertebrae up from mine. The swelling then went all the way up to C2. He spent eighteen months in hospital, was permanently paralysed from the neck down, and still needs a ventilator to breathe.

After he left hospital, he started the Matt Hampson Foundation, which has raised millions for young people who have been severely injured through sport. His ethos is contained in one simple phrase: Get Busy Living – a mantra I was going to apply to my situation.

Henry Fraser is also someone I'd heard about before my accident. He'd been an academy player at Saracens rugby when, at the age of 17, he had gone on holiday to Portugal. He had run into the sea with his friends, but when he'd dived into the surf, he'd hit his head on a sandbank below. Henry sustained a C3/C4 compression fracture of his spinal cord and spent six months in hospital. He was left permanently paralysed from the top of his shoulders down. It had taken months in hospital for him to learn how to breathe without a ventilator. When he was discharged from hospital, he taught himself how to paint intricate and delicate artwork holding a specially adapted paintbrush in his mouth. He is now a celebrated mouth artist.

Information was one of my lifelines: it armed me against my situation. So I started researching others who had come before me and had made a damn good job of what they'd been left with.

Christopher Reeve was an actor who played Superman back in the Seventies and is probably the most famous quadriplegic. He was 42 when he was involved in a riding accident. His horse had suddenly stopped, and he was thrown forwards, landing head-first on the ground. He sustained a C1/C2 spinal cord injury (it doesn't get any higher on the spine than that). His spinal cord was so badly damaged that his skull was completely severed from his spine for several days. He had gone from being a world-famous actor to being permanently paralysed from the neck down.

I was really interested in reading about how he'd adjusted to his new life. He spoke openly about initially considering suicide and it was actually his actor friend, Robin Williams, who turned him around. Robin Williams entered his room, in full character mode and costume, and pretended to be a doctor who needed to perform a rectal exam. Christopher said it was the first time he had laughed since his accident and he knew then that life was worth living. Christopher was inspired by all the people he met in the spinal unit in hospital. So, when he was discharged, he decided to use his fame to campaign for spinal cord injury research and fundraising. He went on to raise millions through the Christopher & Dana Reeve Foundation.

Another person I learnt about was Kirsty Ennis who had joined the Marines when she was just 17. Whilst on her second tour of Afghanistan, the helicopter she was travelling in crashed. She suffered multiple injuries including a traumatic brain injury, spinal injury, extensive damage to her jaw and the eventual amputation of her left leg above the knee. After a year of rehab, she learnt how to walk again using a prosthetic. She was retired from the Marines on medical grounds and started looking around at what else she could do. She started by competing in the Paralympics as a snowboarder, then she walked one thousand miles across the UK to raise money for a non-profit organisation and rounded it all off by working as a stuntwoman in Hollywood. But that wasn't enough. She decided that she wanted to raise money for non-profit organisations by climbing the Seven Summits, which are the highest peaks on each continent. When I learnt about her, she had already conquered Mount Kilimanjaro and was prepping for Carstensz in Oceania.

As I lay in my bed late at night, only using my voice to control my iPad, I thought of Stephen Hawking, so started researching him as well. At the age of 21, he had been diagnosed with motor neurone disease and given just two years to live. Motor neurone disease is a particularly nasty degenerative disease, which, bit by bit, took the movement from his body. He outlived his doctors' prognoses and, at the age of 23 and using a walking stick to steady himself, he married. He went on to have three children. Always fighting against the amount of time he had been given to live, he went on to become one of the twentieth century's most eminent scientists, whose theorems changed the course of cosmology and theoretical physics.

The creeping paralysis first left him unable to walk. A few years later he could only move his fingers and his face, and then, because of medical complications, it took his speech. By the end of his life he communicated through a single muscle in his cheek, which was interpreted by a computer that gave him his iconic voice. He died at the age of 76 – fifty-three years longer than doctors had initially predicted.

Reading about Stephen Hawking was very humbling. For years he watched movement leave his body, knowing it would never return. At least I could watch some movement return to my body, knowing that there might be more to come.

These were just a few of the people I looked up to. They had also suffered unexpected accidents or illnesses and had come out the other side fighting.

I tell myself that, whatever situation I may be facing, there will be someone else who has been through something similar. That I should find them, read about them, and see how they approached it. There is no need to start from the beginning when facing change. Instead, stand on the shoulders of giants.

I stared out of the window in my hospital room. The tantalising view over north Bristol towards Wales was beginning to frustrate me as I hadn't been outside in ten days. I tried to remind myself that I was lucky to have a window; many of the other patients didn't.

'We have to think of his mental health as well as the physical,' my dad said, shifting his weight onto his left leg. He had been making his case for a while and I wasn't sure whether any progress had been made.

My new doctor sighed. 'Let's at least wait until he has been discharged from intensive care.'

Dad had been trying to secure a trip outside in the hospital grounds for me for days. We hadn't told the doctor that I'd already had my jaunt to Costa Coffee as we didn't want to risk getting anyone into trouble.

'We should take a holistic approach,' Dad continued. 'Treat the mind as well as the body.'

'Holistic' – excellent word, Dad. Another thing that I was incredibly grateful for was that my dad, who used to work as a GP, stood a better chance of pushing my case. He understood medical jargon and knew the right points to raise.

The doctor glanced up to the ceiling. He seemed to be weighing everything up. 'I can't promise anything, but I'll speak to my colleagues about it.'

'That's what you said yesterday.'

'I'm sorry, but it's the best I can do.'

The doctor turned to leave.

Dad glanced over as a frown settled on my face. 'I'll be back in a bit, Ed.'

Twenty minutes later, Dad returned. 'They're going to take you outside this afternoon.'

I stared at him before speaking. 'How . . . how? What did you say?'

'What was necessary.'

I gave a joyous whoop – a small victory had been won, but I knew that ultimately everyone was pushing in the same direction. I made a quick call to Lois and arranged to meet her outside in an hour.

Dad never did reveal what he'd said to convince the doctor to let me go outside for fifteen minutes.

That afternoon, I took my second journey out of my room. This time, when we passed through the cardiology ward, I tried to make eye contact and smiled at everyone.

Ten minutes later, the automatic exit doors eased their way open. Lois was standing on the other side of the car park, waiting for me. The first thing I noticed was the light breeze on my skin. It made my arms prickle and goose bumps began to form. I loved this automatic reaction my body had managed to conjure.

My main view was of the sky and I watched the clouds, plump and docile, resting above me. As I was wheeled into the car park, I could hear Lois's approach with two other friends I wasn't expecting. I hadn't known that she was bringing them with her; this had obviously been planned with my dad.

Molly, my 10-year-old boxer, was scooped up into the air and we came face to face. She recognised me instantly and was wriggling to get onto my bed. I lifted my fingers to Molly's fur, and she gave my hand a long lick. I could feel the coarseness of her tongue across parts of my skin. I then reached out and managed to give my other dog, Barry, the smallest of tickles behind his ear with my two working fingers. Fifteen minutes with my dogs – it was bliss.

Animals don't see you as any different. They don't stare at your neck brace or try to hold back the tears. They just recognise the person they share a home with.

This lovely bit of normality in an alien world settled me for the rest of the day and I slept well that night. Whether it's a favourite meal, looking at some old photos or a trip to see the dogs, it's important to keep some normality in your life.

I knew it was mine. I knew how you were supposed to move it. I knew what it felt like to move it. But it just didn't want to play ball.

It was a very unnerving experience staring at a part of your body, telling it to move, and it deciding not to respond. Despite this, I had spent every waking hour of the last two days staring at my feet and telling them to move. Never has a toe been watched so intensely and it was beginning to shrivel under my stern gaze.

I changed tactics and began talking to my toes. Words of encouragement, cajoling, bribery, a stream of abuse and even the occasional apology. Nothing worked.

It was my twelfth day in hospital. Lois was sitting next to me, pulling her long, blonde hair into a messy topknot and then repeating the process when she didn't like the way that it sat.

'I think I'll have to go back to Cardiff tomorrow. Just for the day,' she said. 'I have to check on the house; we haven't been there for ages.'

Since my accident, Lois had been staying at my dad and stepmum's house, as it was much closer to the hospital. I didn't know why, but the idea of Lois going back to Cardiff, even for a day, unsettled me. It was as if life was starting to shift back to some semblance of normality for everyone, apart from me.

'Do you have to go back already?' I said, still firing those messages to my toe. 'Can't it wait a week?'

'Not really, Ed. I have to say something to work as well, I've been off for nearly two weeks. They'll want to know when I'll be coming back.'

My stomach dropped at the thought of Lois and my family returning to their lives, while I lay in hospital, static, unmoving. I told myself that's what people have to do in these situations. Lois was right to want to go and check on the house; we couldn't just let it sit there.

'What time do you think you'll go?'

'Probably around— Ed, did you just move your toe?'

'What?'

I stared at her.

'Do it again . . . Again.'

Another message was shot down.

'Oh!' Lois said, standing up. 'It moved. It definitely moved!'

I stared at it; there was a definite twitch.

Terrified that it might stop moving, I kept trying to wiggle my toe as Lois ran to get my mum.

All bets were off. Everything I had been told was now out of the window. I'd sent a message to the furthest point from my brain. There was life in my legs . . . it might not be much, but it was all the hope I needed.

CHAPTER 4

THE 'F' WORD

All I could do was watch as Lois systematically organised the belongings in my room. She was now crouched in the corner, folding my clothes. They didn't really need tidying, but she obviously felt the need to do something practical. I understood that – I was desperate to do anything that didn't involve lying flat on my back . . .

Shit. I was crying again.

I quickly blinked away the tears before Lois saw.

Why did I keep on doing this? I'd never really cried before the accident. I had nothing against crying; it just wasn't something I did. I'm not saying that I was an emotionally stunted, manly-man who went around headbutting walls. Instead, I just got on with things. I processed them in my own way. But I couldn't seem to do that at the moment, and I didn't know why.

For three days I'd had a toe that wiggled and a finger I could now type with. Shouldn't I be on top of the world?

You also have a body that doesn't move, and you don't know when this will end. Or if it ever will . . .

My thoughts had turned against me these last two

days. I couldn't stop thinking the worst things about myself; I would never have had those thoughts about someone else in my position.

'Ed,' Lois said, while balling some socks, 'what do you think I should do about my job?'

'Umm . . .' I responded, testing my voice to make sure it sounded normal. 'I don't know, whatever you want to do.'

'And netball, too,' she continued, still crouching over my suitcase.

'You've been doing a lot of thinking,' I said. 'You haven't mentioned any of this before.'

'I've been thinking lots about the practical stuff. It's how my brain works, you know that. I've got about eighteen steps in my head and I'm wondering which one I should tackle first.'

'Well, what else is there?' I asked, reasonably sure I'd got control of myself again.

'I've been thinking about the house. It's not really very practical with all those stairs. I'm not even sure if we'll go back to Cardiff.'

I flinched. Not go back to Cardiff? What did she think was going to happen to us?

She stood up and stretched before turning around. I eyed her ease of movement and for the first time I was jealous of it.

'I think I'd like to go back to work one day a week, just as a trial,' she said, now circling her arms behind her back to free up her muscles. 'And start playing netball again. What do you think?'

Before I knew it, I was crying again. Big wet tears that no one could hide were streaming down my face. I felt a surge of anger that I could lose control like that.

'Ed, what's wrong?' Lois asked, hurrying over to the bed.

I gasped in air, unable to answer, just wanting the simple dignity of being able to wipe my face. But no, I just had to lie there, unable to even turn away.

'It's starting to feel like you're not there for me,' I eventually said between sobs. 'You're busy planning what you're going to do next and I'm just lying here.'

Lois's face crumpled. We never argued; we weren't that type of couple.

'Oh, Ed,' she said. 'I'm so sorry. I can't believe that I'm here thinking about netball and wor—'

'Knock, knock,' one of the nurses said from the open doorway.

We both stopped and stared over to her. Couldn't she tell this wasn't a good time?

'I'm sorry,' the nurse continued, smiling apologetically. 'I've left it as long as I could but visiting hours ended ten minutes ago.'

'Can I stay tonight?' Lois asked. 'Could you make an exception this one time? Ed's not in a good way . . .' She gave a furtive glance over in my direction.

'I'm so sorry, guys,' the nurse said, 'but the rules are the rules. No overnight stays, whatever the circumstances. We'll take good care of him. I promise.'

After Lois left, I stared at the door she'd just walked through. I had to deal with the next twelve hours by myself. How had I gone from nearly two weeks of positivity, to this?

The silence of my empty room refused to provide an answer.

'Alexa,' I said. 'Play *Rumours* by Fleetwood Mac.'

My Amazon Dot responded to my request, and the familiar chords of 'Songbird' floated out of the speaker. For some reason, this album had been constantly on my mind since my accident.

I'd never been a huge Fleetwood Mac fan before, but now it was my saviour at times.

I'd barely slept the night before; the unwelcome thoughts had taunted me, tested me, before going for the jugular. I was physically and emotionally exhausted. The back of my head and neck ached constantly and I couldn't remember the last time I had felt comfortable lying in my hospital bed. Despite this, sheer exhaustion and the floating voice of Stevie Nicks singing 'Dreams' carried me off into a disjointed sleep. I slipped away for a moment . . .

I was in a park with my friends. We had been throwing a ball around and the accident had never happened. I dived full stretch to my right, almost had it . . .

I woke with a start. Looking around, it took me a second to remember why I was in hospital. I was still in my intensive care bed, but the echoes of my dream had stayed with me. I stared up at the ceiling as I tried to calm my heart. My subconscious was still too close; I would slip back into the dream and have to remind myself about the accident all over again.

I stared around my room, looking for something to distract me from replaying the conversation I'd just had with Lois. Why had I been such an idiot with her? I didn't recognise that man. A low feeling of dread began to coil its way around me. Did I really think that she wasn't there for me, just because she wanted to talk about our future together? Christ, she'd been in the hospital *every* single day since my accident.

Why would I say that to her?

I tried to look at it objectively, like the old me would have done.

My initial sadness, anger and desperation had almost sub-sided. Instead, the 'F' word was everywhere. Everything about my current situation was frustrating. The claustrophobia, the pain, the lack of sleep, the constant medical observations . . . even getting frustrated was frustrating. I suppose I'm quite a proud person and this sudden loss of dignity over the last two weeks had begun to wear me down. *Bowel Care and Bed Baths* – that would be the name of the musical production of this period of my life. I'd never imagined that at the age of 28 I'd be in this position, reliant on a team of nurses to carry out functions that most people don't even think about. That proud, independent, young man had gone. Who was left?

For a moment I danced on the edge of something, a brief flit into one of my many possible futures. Me, bitter and aggrieved, wronging others because I thought that I had the right to. Hadn't I suffered? Hadn't I been through the worst? I would justify the wrongness of my actions by what had happened to me.

No. That wasn't the way I wanted to live.

I thought about what my friend, Tom, who had died nearly five years ago would do if he knew I'd got myself into this state. He had loved life; lived and breathed for the next adventure. He was also tough. Tom never took the knocks personally, never let himself wallow in self-pity. It didn't take long to realise that he'd tell me to sort myself out and look to the future.

I had to go back to basics: knowledge, distractions and learning from others.

I started up my iPad and said aloud what I was feeling. I'd found that this was by far the best distraction I had during the long nights. When I had finished, I read over some of what I'd said:

Losing your independence is shit. In hospital you have to leave your pride at the door, and at a time when you are at your most vulnerable. I'm sure there are lots of people who would love the idea of being fed grapes whilst having their feet rubbed. But when it's happening because you can't physically do it yourself, it doesn't quite carry the same allure. Mundane everyday tasks that I once took for granted are all of a sudden either impossible or so hard they make me want to throw myself out of the window. As I was physically unable to throw myself out of the window, I have decided to take on as many of these mundane tasks as possible. This might result in a neck brace full of food, a straw in the eye or a mouthful of envelope. But how are you supposed to improve without giving it a go?

I had to start fighting the negativity again. Somehow, without me even noticing, I'd given up. These last two days have been really bad, but I had the chance to change. I hadn't come this far to pick a future that I didn't want to live.

The next morning, I felt a calmness within me that I hadn't felt for days. I couldn't control my body, but I was in control of my greatest resource at this time: my mind.

While I waited for Lois to arrive, I practised tapping the fingers on my right hand, one after the other, as if I were playing a scale on a piano that no one else could hear.

At exactly 8 a.m., Lois walked into my room and tentatively waved at me from the doorway. I looked over and took a moment to enjoy the sight of her. She had come back.

She shut the door behind her and walked over to my bed. I tried to speak but she cut me off. 'Ed, I wanted to say I'm sorry for talking about all that stuff yesterday. You've been doing so well that I sometimes forget that you might be worrying about things more than you let on.'

I smiled at her. 'You've stolen my apology thunder. I had it all planned out. There was a lengthy monologue, even an interval.'

Lois laughed and the tension lifted.

'Look at this,' I said, showing her my tapping fingers.

Lois bent down and peered at them. 'The middle and little fingers are definitely moving more.'

I watched a small frown settle on her features as she studied my fingers. She treated them as if they were most important things in the world.

I took a deep breath. 'You didn't need to apologise. It's me who should be doing that. I'm sorry for being an idiot and I don't really think you're not there for me. I promise I won't question it again.'

She smiled at me. 'I think that's the sincerest apology you've ever given me.'

I raised my eyebrows in mock protest. 'I think this calls for a celebration. Alexa play—'

'Not Fleetwood Mac again!'

'Nooo, Lois. I'm not that predictable.' I tutted. 'Alexa, play *Legend* by Bob Marley.'

Lois let out a groan as 'Is this Love' started up.

I didn't care that it was the fourth time this week, I bloody loved this album. I bopped my eyebrows along to the reggae beats.

Lois frowned. 'Alexa, stop.'

Nothing happened.

'Alexa, stop playing *Legend* by Bob Marley.'

Nothing. This was the thing I loved about Alexa. She wouldn't respond to Lois's requests, which I found hilarious.

'Alexa really is your favourite person,' Lois said, sitting down in the chair next to me.

'*Could you be looooved?*' I sang. 'Are you jealous of Alexa, Lois?'

'Course not. It's just annoying that she only responds to you.'

Lois kicked off her trainers and rested her feet on the edge of my bed. She had settled in for the day.

I smiled at her, content, as I tapped my fingers along to the music.

It's important to recognise that we all have bad days. It's normal for life to get a bit too much at times and for our initial reaction to be negative. What's more important is how we continue to react. If we can, we should try not to pass on our negativity to those around us. I know this is hard and we all fall down on this. An apology can often repair some of the damage, and we shouldn't fudge it by adding an excuse at the end.

People will try to help you during a time of change or crisis, and you'll be surprised by how wide your support network actually is. But only a few of those people will stick around if you constantly push them away.

I don't think I would have made it this far if it wasn't for the people around me. I didn't really appreciate the support network I had until it was called into action. The lengths that my family, friends and even strangers have gone to make this journey that little bit easier for me was overwhelming. I had been so lucky that between my oversized family, Lois and my friends, I was rarely alone during the day. The silver lining of this accident was that I got to spend quality time with the people I loved, not just a hasty pint or a lunch that was shoehorned in between other meetings. Instead, I've had time to talk to the people I care about, not even about important things, or deep, life-changing conversations; just the lovely mundanities of life that we can laugh at together. I'm grateful for this time that I have been given with them.

In turn, I knew I wanted to repay that support, whether I regained any more movement or not. I'm a firm believer that what goes around, comes around. And I was lucky to have a lot of support to repay.

It had been sixteen days since my accident and my right side continued to make progress. Each day had brought a little more movement and sensation. Sometimes, the movement on my right side only accentuated the lack of movement on my left, which stubbornly refused to budge. Not even the twitch of a finger. When faced with the daunting prospect of lasting limitation, the want for more had become a daily emotional struggle. I knew that this desire was a ridiculous notion and I would therefore try to distract my thoughts away from it. I would spend my evenings learning about the people who had come before me. This had helped me realise that any progress, even if it was exclusively on one side, was a blessing and shouldn't be a source of frustration. I needed to keep on reminding myself that I was doing okay. I had to focus on the process, not the outcome.

It was late morning and Lois and my dad had been sitting with me when my doctor entered the room.

'Ed, how are you feeling today?'

'Pretty good, I can almost hold something with the fingers on my right hand now.' I frowned. 'Well, if it's the perfect size and it's placed inside of them . . . But it's still progress.'

I gave a demonstration and he nodded appreciatively.

'Excellent. I've also got some news for you. We've managed to secure you a bed in the neurology ward at Bath hospital. We'll arrange for an ambulance to take you there tomorrow.'

All three of us started talking at once. This is what we'd been hoping for; moving out of intensive care would be a huge leap forwards. The two-hourly checks should be reduced and changing hospitals meant I'd only be a few miles from my dad's house so they wouldn't have to travel so far to visit me. Best of all, I'd hopefully be able to start some rehab. I'd been reading up about what types of rehab other quadriplegics had found helpful, such as hydrotherapy and a tilt table. But I couldn't explore any of their suggestions whilst I was still in intensive care.

'I'll go and get your mum and tell her the news,' Dad said.

'We'd better get packing, then,' Lois added, as she surveyed my room. Despite her best efforts to keep it ordered, there was no denying that I'd accumulated a lot of stuff. Everyone who had visited had brought gifts or bits of equipment that they thought might help with my recovery. I stared at the three juggling balls that were resting on top of two stacked hampers of food and smiled.

'Don't forget Alexa,' I said to Lois. 'I don't want her to go "accidentally" missing in the move.'

'Hmmm . . .' was the only response that I got.

A few hours later, my room had been packed up and I'd settled into my last night in intensive care. I'd be lying if I said that I would miss it, but that didn't change how grateful I was to everyone at Southmead Hospital who had looked after me. From Mr Barua who had saved my spinal cord, to the nurses who'd jollied me along and tried to make bowel care and bed baths as normal as they possibly could, to the volunteer guitar player who'd come in every week and spent his spare time serenading the patients ('play "The Chain" by Fleetwood Mac again!').

All of them deserved my thanks.

Fifty years ago, it's likely I wouldn't have survived my accident. The huge advances in medical science have helped with that.

Seventy-five years ago, with a lesser injury, I wouldn't have survived as there was no NHS. There wouldn't have been a reliable ambulance service to collect me and take me to hospital (what existed before 1948 was an ambulance service that wasn't available to everyone). Even if I had managed to make it to a hospital, I would've had to pay for all of my care and at some point my money would have run out. And then what?

Alternatively, if we had a health insurance scheme in the UK, rather than the NHS, I might have survived my accident but I'd be paying for it another way. I've read about the difficulties that people in my position have faced when trying to reinsure themselves after their health insurance premium ran out. They often struggled to find insurance for a reasonable cost as their spinal-cord injury would be classed as a pre-existing injury. I'm therefore eternally grateful that this little island I live on decided to provide free national healthcare.

I tried to remember how lucky I was that my life had been saved several times in the first few days following my accident. My dad and Diane were my first saviours; they stopped me from being moved and knew to keep my spine straight. The ambulance people, and the doctor with them, had finely balanced the urgent need to get me to hospital with keeping me alive along the way. Mr Barua and his team gave my body the chance to heal and the nurses kept me alive in the following days when I was unable to move or feed myself. So I knew that, despite everything I'd gone through, I couldn't get frustrated with my situation. I owed it to all those people who'd helped me. The 'F' word could bugger off for a bit.

CHAPTER 5

ON TOUR

I'd said my goodbyes to the nurses who were working that morning and they'd wished me all the best for my stay in Bath hospital. As I waited for the ambulance to arrive, my excitement growing for the next stage of my recovery, one of the nurses popped her head around the door.

'I've only just got on shift and they tell me you're leaving!' she said, still standing in the doorway.

'I know, it was news to me too. I can't wait to get over there and start on my physio.'

She leant against the glass section of the wall, all shiny and new. It still felt like I'd spent the last two weeks on the set of an American hospital drama.

'I bet you can't wait to get going. And you'll be in safe hands there; it's the ward where Pete Bishop is the head neuro-physiotherapist.'

My ears pricked up. 'You've heard of him?'

'Oh yes, he's a bit of a legend. From Sicily, I think, and ex-army.'

I let out a low whistle as images of a battle-hardened,

ex-Mafia kingpin, neuro-physiotherapist rushed through my mind. This was the man for me.

Travelling in the ambulance, the journey wasn't quite the high-speed delivery that I had been expecting. The lights were flashing but I was a bit disappointed that there was no siren. As we pootled along on the inside lane of the dual carriageway that connects Bristol to Bath, I realised this wasn't the emergency affair I'd anticipated because they wanted to make sure that there was no damage to my spinal cord on the way there. Fair play to them – it would be a pretty bad day at the office if they delivered me with less spinal cord than they'd collected me with.

I spent the journey trying to distract myself from the bumps in the road by chatting to the paramedic in the back with me. Every jolt made me panic that the 4mm of spinal cord I had left was being whittled away. Unable to see out of the small window, I played a game of trying to guess the route the ambulance was taking just by the frequency of the familiar roundabouts and turns that we made.

Pulling up at the Royal United Hospital in Bath, I couldn't help but think back to when another set of ambulance doors had opened and I'd been wheeled out under the same entrance-way sign. Like then, it was a warm day, and I savoured the glimpse of light-blue sky, so pale it was almost white in places. God, I missed being outside.

All too quickly, I was wheeled into the entrance. The clank of my trolley as it travelled over the lip made me wince. I squeezed my eyes shut as I thought about that frail length of spinal cord that connected my brain to the rest of my body. Every bump of the trolley as it travelled through the maze of corridors made me grit my teeth. To distract myself I opened my eyes, stared up at the ceiling and tried to take my focus away from my physical state and shift it on to my external surroundings.

There was no towering glass ceiling here. Instead, I was met with grey tiles that sagged in places. A few were missing altogether and wires spilled out from their yawning gaps – was that safe? I had been born in this hospital, had visited it numerous times in my clumsy teenage years, so I was familiar with it. But I'd never spent much time looking at it from this angle. It didn't appear that they'd had the funds to do any updates since I'd been born; there was no multi-million-pound refurbishment that I could see. I began to feel a little nervous about my transfer. Was this the best place for me?

Arriving at Helena Ward, I tried to smile as I was greeted by the friendly nursing team who announced that they'd been saving the end bed on the ward for me. This was a coveted position as you were only directly next to one of your seven fellow patients. I thanked them and tried to smile at Lois, Mum and Dad. They'd arrived before me and had tried to give the end bed a homely feeling by depositing all of my belongings around it. Lois caught my eye and a message passed between us. I knew then that we were both worried about my transfer to this hospital.

The curtain next to my neighbour was pulled shut and it bulged outwards as hampers, a suitcase and a couple of bags of fresh food infringed onto his side of the partition – if he wanted to take up a boundary dispute with me, he'd have had a good case.

The nursing team transferred me into my new bed and we all politely tried to ignore the man across from me who kept on shouting out random words. That's the thing about a neurology ward, it isn't just for people like me with spinal injuries. It's for people with brain injuries as well, and they could be at any stage in their recovery.

Mum pulled the other curtain closed and we tried to carry on as if I was still in my room for one at Southmead Hospital. Naturally our voices were lowered and there were obviously some topics we skirted around as we were very aware that a thin piece of plastic may have given the illusion of privacy, but the reality was very different. We might as well have asked the other patients and nursing staff to pull up a chair.

Lois jumped as the curtain next to her was pulled back briskly. We all looked around guiltily, worried in case we'd broken Helena Ward etiquette so early on in my stay. Maybe we should have left the curtain open . . .

A five-foot-four, stocky man with dark, gelled hair stood on the other side of the curtain. He was dressed head to toe in Fila sportswear and his trousers were tucked into ankle-high army boots.

'You must be Ed,' he said in a thick West Country accent. He looked me up and down. 'Big lad, aren't you?'

'Not as big as I used to be. Turns out lying on your back all day isn't too great for muscle wastage.'

He nodded. 'We'll see what we can do about that. I'm Pete; I'll be your physio while you're with us.'

He wasn't exactly what I'd been expecting, but I was so pleased to meet someone who I could start working with on my recovery. Everyone introduced themselves and Pete made an effort to put us all at ease.

'We'll start with the ASIA testing on Monday,' Pete said. 'And we'll get going with you then.'

'Maybe we could do it now?' I said. 'Mum and Dad can shift over and I want to talk to you about these studies I've read from Japan—'

'We can talk about what you've read while I assess you on Monday. I'd be really interested to hear about them then.'

'Perhaps we can run through a few moves today,' I said. 'So I've got something to do over the weekend. I was think—'

'Ah, Ed,' Dad said, 'you might want to look at the time.'

I checked my iPad. It was after six. And it was a Friday. Outside of intensive care, all hospitals sort of shut down over the weekend. They operate on a strict nine to five and I'd already been infringing on Pete's time. I'd have to be patient and wait another two days to get started.

Up until now, I've spared the details of what some of the side effects of a spinal cord injury are. In the early weeks, there were more important things for me to worry about, and soon the daily bed baths, bowel evacuations and catheter checks had become normal. This was partially because this intimate care is normal to the medical staff. Back in Bristol, I'd followed their lead and we had fallen into a sustainable, but perhaps not always physically comfortable, routine.

Imagine now that you have just met a room full of new people. You want to fit in, you want them to like you and you understand that first impressions count. Now imagine that some of the things they need to do in your initial twenty-four hours together is stick their fingers up your bum, wash your entire body and fiddle around with your todger as they check whether your catheter is working. Sort of puts you on the back foot, doesn't it?

Because that's what happens with spinal injuries. It's not

all long-distance shots of you lying on a bed, gazing out of the window, brow puckered as you wonder when you will next feel the sun on your skin. Instead, the camera is up close; you're worried that you haven't showered for two weeks and it can frequently be very personal. Not only have you lost the movement in your arms so you can't wash yourself, but you also have several important messages that are trying to travel down your spinal cord but can't reach the right station.

The first is to your bladder. The sphincter muscle that controls the release of urine from the bladder is rendered useless, which is really common for people with spinal cord injuries. Sometimes, it is left loose so you have no control over when you pee, but more commonly it is left shut and the messages from your brain are unable to tell your bladder it's full and should open. If your bladder overfills it will stretch, leaving permanent damage, and it can also cause serious problems with your kidneys. I was still under anaesthetic when my catheter was inserted so I didn't feel anything, but every day nurses would have to collect the bags of pee I produced and often check that the catheter was in place and clean.

The second, even more personal issue, is bowel management. Following a serious spinal cord injury, a lot of people are unable to poo for lengths of time and digestion takes a lot longer as well. So, every morning I would have a suppository popped up my bum and also a nurse would try to use their finger to pull the sluggish deposits from inside me. All the jokes my mates used to bandy about concerning gloved doctors and prostrate examinations had become a daily experience. The cherry on top was that the nurses would then inspect what had come out of me and record its consistency by comparing it to the coincidently, but aptly named, 'Bristol Stool Scale'.

Dignity . . . window . . .

I knew that it would become just another part of my daily routine once I got used to the nursing team, but in those early days I had to find a quick way of relaxing. The ability to switch off is very important when you need to leave your body for a bit. Distractions and refocusing your thoughts are always a winner but, for a quick fix, I like to take myself away with some music – the ultimate, instantaneous focus shifter.

That's when I came up with the brand-new, soon to be charting, Spotify playlist: 'Top five songs to have your bowels evacuated to.'

And, like all good playlists, it has a start, middle and end. You're welcome.

1. 'Help!', The Beatles
2. 'Under Pressure', Queen and David Bowie
3. 'Hold Back the River', James Bay
4. 'Landslide', Fleetwood Mac
5. 'All Right Now', Free

You may think my music choices suck and a bit of thrash metal is what gets you to that better place. But that's the point. Make a playlist of your own that you can't help but tap your finger to. Unashamedly use those songs, laugh at your situation and squeeze every bit of mood-boosting joy out of them. They're not a long-term fix, but they can be a very welcome plaster when they're needed.

I would like to say that the next morning I'd woken up with the same positivity I'd left Southmead Hospital with, but one of my worst nights of sleep had put a dampener on my spirits.

Firstly, plastic curtains do not block sound. I might as well have been sharing a large bed with seven other men. There was the expected snoring and checks on each of us at all hours. But there was something else as well. A couple of these guys had sustained recent brain injuries and I'd never experienced what effect this can have on people. They were distraught, crying out in the night, confused. It was immensely saddening that they had to face the struggle of finding their way back alone. It helped to put my own concerns into perspective. At least following my accident I was still me. A vertically challenged, four-finger tapping me, but my mind was still rooting for me.

After I'd listened to my new playlist and tried to make polite conversation with the nurse who'd given me my morning once over, I was pleased to see Lois and my dad appear early. Over the course of the morning a steady stream of visitors arrived. They were mainly local friends who hadn't been able to make it over to Bristol regularly so wanted to make up for it by popping in at the weekend. Unlike intensive care, which was serious in nature, Helena Ward had a much more relaxed vibe, possibly induced by the mid-spring heatwave that was starting up. Here, I was allowed unlimited visitors and there weren't the same restrictions on visiting times.

A few hours later, the ward matron came over to my bed.

'This isn't really working, is it?' she said, hands on hips.

I silently agreed. I had kept on trying to reassure myself that this hospital stay was only temporary. I was only here while I waited for a place to open up at a specialist spinal unit in Salisbury.

All eleven of us looked up at her guiltily. We had been making a fair bit of a racket and four of my friends had to sit on other people's knees as we'd run out of chairs. The physio equipment my visitors had brought in with them that morning was teetering in a corner and had infringed even further into my neighbours' space.

The matron looked around at us all and then broke into a smile. 'We have a side room that's become available. If you all pitch in, we'll get you over there by the afternoon.'

With an air of excitement, everyone grabbed a bag, apart from me of course. I contributed by managing to stop my headphones from sliding off the bed with two of the working fingers on my right hand. The nursing team then shifted into action and we were off.

Two hours later we were all settled in. I was now the proud occupant of one of the larger side rooms, which had high ceilings and two big windows. Granted, it also had bright lavender, chipped paint and three missing ceiling tiles, but it was mine. I knew straight away how lucky I was as it offered the possibility of some peace and quiet and the chance to relax.

After the initial excitement, everyone could see how tired I was. So, one by one, my mates said their farewells and promised to come back the following week. The sun was blazing and my room had begun to heat up. Without noticing it, I fell asleep.

I woke up still feeling groggy. Glancing towards the window, I realised that a few hours must have passed as the sun was much farther across on its travels. Lois was sitting in the corner of the room looking at her phone. I was surprised to see my mate, Will, sitting on the chair next to me. He must have arrived after I had fallen asleep. He was reading something on my iPad, which normally sat on the stand that hovered above my bed.

'Good to see you, Will. Have you been here long?' My voice was sluggish and my mouth dried out from the heat.

He looked up. 'A couple of hours. Thought I'd wait to see if you woke up.'

I put my one working index finger to good use and pointed at the iPad. 'What are you reading about?'

'I was having a look through that diary you've been keeping about your injury.' He shifted forwards on his chair. As a prop for the Wasps rugby team, he was a big man and the chair squeaked in protest. 'Two things. One – you're fucking weird. Two – you should make this public. It could help someone.'

I tried to process what he was saying before responding. 'Two things. One – didn't your mum teach you that diaries are private. Two – no one wants to read my ramblings. I was just keeping it to help me get to sleep.'

Lois looked up. 'Will's right, Ed. You should share it. There's some great stuff in there.'

I stared at Lois.

'Have you read my diary too, Lois?'

At least she had the decency to blush.

'Maybe. Only once or twice, though.'

I sighed. 'Anyone else read it?'

Lois stood up and came over to the bed. 'Maybe your step-brother, Chris, when he was looking for a film . . .'

It was at times like this that I wanted to roll over and turn my back on everyone. Instead, I had to settle with a loud huffing noise.

'Think about it,' Will said, leaning forwards, 'you could help people who are facing a long stay in hospital. You know, tricks of the trade. That sort of thing.'

'I suppose so,' I said, reluctantly. 'I'll have to give it a bit of thought.'

'I've got some news that will cheer you up,' Lois said, bouncing on her feet. 'The nurses said that we can bring food in from the local restaurants. I was thinking—'

'A roast from GPT?' My mood had suddenly lifted. 'With extra colly cheese?'

'And extra crackling,' Lois responded.

She knew me well.

On Monday morning, Pete was by my bedside at 9 a.m. on the dot, wearing a Kappa T-shirt and a big smile.

I'd had a rough night as I'd knocked the buzzer off my bed and had needed the cough machine to clear my chest. It didn't feel like I was drowning like it had back in Southmead Hospital, but it was still very uncomfortable. Unable to call out for a nurse, I'd had to wait an hour until someone passed by and heard my gurgling. I had coped with the hour by practising mindfulness and concentrating on my breathing. It hadn't helped to clear my lungs, but it had helped prevent me from spiralling into panic.

'So, we're going to do your ASIA tests and then make a plan,' Pete said.

'Sounds good to me.'

Off he went – pulling, pressing, watching.

He finished off by scratching the bottom of my foot, like my friend, Murph, used to do for hours back in Southmead Hospital. My leg jerked upward in its automatic response.

'That must be a good sign,' I said.

'It is and it isn't.'

'Do it again.'

'I shouldn't really,' Pete replied. 'It will only reinforce the automatic response. You have to be careful with it and only do it a few times.'

I thought back guiltily to all the hours my friend, Murph, had spent scratching the bottom of my foot. I really hoped we hadn't done any permanent damage.

Half an hour later, Pete had the results. 'Well, it's better than last time. There's a bit more sensation in your right hand but still no grip strength. And, of course, there's no movement at all on your left side. According to the ASIA test, it's still unlikely that you'll walk again. I imagine it's not the news you were hoping for.'

'Even with my moving toe?'

'Even with your moving toe.'

I tried to process what he was saying as he slung the clipboard onto the end of my bed.

'But what do they know, eh?' Pete continued. 'I think we'll have you up and about in no time.'

I stared at him. 'Really?'

This was the first time anyone involved in my care had said this.

'Yes, and I'm going to do everything to help you get there. We'll start with trying to get you to sit up.'

I grinned at him. 'So far the majority of my rehab has revolved around trying to pick things up and occasionally throw them at people. I think I'm ready for something a bit more constructive.'

Sitting up was not going to be as simple as Pete and a couple of nurses hauling my top half upwards and quickly stuffing a few pillows behind me. Instead, my bed would have to be raised by a few degrees over the next two days for a couple of hours each time. If they had sat me up straight away I would have passed out. This was because I'd been flat on my back for three weeks and my body had forgotten how to regulate my blood pressure. I'd already been raised to twenty degrees in Southmead, but it was time to push it a bit further.

As Pete pressed the button on the side of my bed and the top half of it slowly raised, I began to feel dizzy, my head swirling as if I could feel the blood moving through it like waves. He stopped for a moment and we waited for the threat of me fainting to clear. I was no longer looking directly at a ceiling; instead I could see the top part of the wall – I wanted more! As soon as I was ready, he pressed it again and I came up further until he stopped it halfway.

Forty-five degrees. It might not sound much to anyone else, but it gave me a whole new perspective. For a start, I wasn't looking directly up Pete's nose any more, which was the main viewpoint I'd had of all my visitors up until now. When I was able to fully sit up, it would also allow me to eat a meal with less chance of choking and begin my first proper physio sessions. I had a new short-term goal to aim for.

That evening, after everyone had gone, I looked back at one of the most productive days I'd had since my accident. Okay, forty-five degrees was a pretty slouchy way of sitting up and you wouldn't do it in the office, but it was halfway to fully sitting up, and I believed that with Pete (literally) behind me, I could achieve it.

I hadn't felt this hopeful in a while and it made me think of everyone else lying in their hospital beds around the country. How were they doing right now?

My friend Will might have been right: perhaps I could

help a couple of patients who had just arrived in intensive care or a neurological ward. Perhaps I should give it a go. Turning on my iPad, I thought about what I should say. Lois had suggested I post the first blog on Instagram as I already had an account and a few of my friends might share it, which would give it a chance of reaching the people who most needed it. It seemed like a good suggestion.

I opened up my account and scrolled through what I'd posted that year. Four posts in four months. And one of them was a photo of a highland cow. Hardly the stuff of social media influencers.

I sighed. This was way out of my comfort zone, showing any sort of vulnerability or weakness had always been frowned upon in my rugby career. Would this even reach the people who might need it?

Well, no one's going to see it if you don't post anything.

Good point, well made.

But where to start?

At the beginning. And maybe with an introduction to your-self.

The only option I had was to tap the post out with the knuckle of my index finger on my right hand as I couldn't straighten the finger enough to use it to type. Although mobile, all of the fingers on my right hand curled around and were clawed. Thirty minutes later I read over what I had written:

On the 8th April at a family friends' BBQ I dived into the shallow end of a swimming pool. After hitting my head on the bottom I realised I couldn't swim to the surface because I'd lost movement in my legs and power in my arms. My dad (a retired GP) and friend Daffyd immediately knew something was wrong, pulled me to the surface and stabilised me in the pool until the ambulance came.

I was transferred to Southmead Hospital with a fracture dislocation at the C6/7 joint. After a number of MRI scans and X-rays the Drs decided to operate at 2 a.m. to stabilise my neck as pressure was being put on my spinal cord. In surgery they removed my shattered disc, relocated my vertebrae and fixed it in place with a metal plate.

I woke up in ICU, luckily completely coherent, however no feeling below my neck other than limited movement in my right arm.

You never think this shit is going to happen to you, but it did, now I've got to deal with it. This is my road to recovery . . .

Before I got the chance to chicken out, I hit 'Share'.

It was done.

CHAPTER 6

THE LONG ROAD

'Come on, ramp it up!' Pete shouted.

The sweat was pouring down me and I gritted my teeth. Engaging what was left of my core muscles, I tried to stabilise my torso with Pete's help.

'Only a bit longer,' Pete exclaimed. 'One more push.'

Anyone who walked past my room would have thought I was giving birth, not trying to stay sitting up for the first time. Pete had me perched on the edge of my bed. Both of my hands were at my side as he knelt behind me and guided me with arms underneath mine. It was at times like this that I realised how disabled I was. I couldn't even stay sitting up by myself; my body threatened to tip me over in every direction.

My muscles juddered in protest, but I ignored the pain and breathed out deeply. I drew on all my reserves and focused on stabilising myself. And then, for three seconds, I was just a man sitting on the edge of his bed. It didn't matter that it was a fleeting moment, it was still my achievement and it felt wonderful. I took a moment to survey my room at this novel ninety-degree angle before Pete lowered me back down.

One thing I will never take for granted again is my core

muscles. It's only when they stopped working that I began to appreciate how integral they are. The accident had switched off the power to the muscles along the left-hand side of my trunk and severely impaired those on the right. The result was a torso with the strength and consistency of a soup sandwich. Sitting, standing, rolling, twisting, coughing, just about everything is only possible with some degree of core strength – it's what holds you together.

Pete leant over me as I grinned up at him. 'Same again tomorrow?'

I loved the physical challenge I was now able to engage in and it was what I had been hankering for back in Southmead Hospital, but I soon realised that every physio session was as much a mental challenge as a physical one. Not being able to do what had come so easily before was frustrating, and if I was honest with myself, quite upsetting. And I'd have to do it all again tomorrow.

My left leg and hand were also causing me a lot of worry as there was still no movement in them. In my darker hours, often in the middle of the night, I wondered if I would regain only the use of one side of my body. Would the muscles in my left leg and arm wither away if I couldn't cajole them into becoming part of my recovery?

As always, I tried to push these worries away by refocusing my thoughts. Now that I could sit up, I was able to be hoisted out of bed and do a bit more about trying to wake my muscles up.

The next morning, Pete wheeled into my room what could only be described as a grandad chair with wheels. It was a cherry-red, high-backed, padded chair – the sort you would see in an old peoples' home – and, in front of it, Pete had placed a machine with two peddles and a monitor.

Behind him was a big guy who looked to be an ex-rugby player himself. He was tall, well-built but didn't have the bravado that so many rugby players have. In fact, he was almost a bit shy.

'This is Wyn,' Pete said. 'He normally does respiratory physio, but I told him about you and he offered to come and help out.'

'That's very kind of you both,' I said. 'And what have you brought with you?'

'Let's get you up and I'll show you.'

There wasn't much I could do to help as Pete and the nurses transferred me onto my new piece of equipment using a hoist. My disability was always clearest when I had to be moved around the room by a small crane. It made me feel helpless.

'It's not the latest model . . .' Pete concluded after I was settled in.

'It looks like it was released the same year as the Sega Mega Drive. Did you just get me out of bed to play Pac-Man?' I added.

Pete grinned. 'No, nothing like that. But it will do the job, now that you've got the power in your right leg to start turning over the peddle.'

The 'MOTOmed' was a power-assisted bike, designed to get your legs moving. Although my left leg was still a passenger, the process would hopefully help maintain some muscle memory so there would be a halt to the wastage on both sides. An hour on my new chair and I returned to bed feeling like I'd actually achieved something. I now had something tangible to do, something to break up the day. Although I was still a long way off from being able to work up a sweat, I was glad to be back on the bike.

That afternoon, my ears pricked up when I heard a different sound in the hallway; it wasn't the usual squeaky trolly or the rubber-soled shoes of the nurses. Instead, it sounded like sharp claws skittering down the hallway. It was what I had been waiting for.

Lois burst into the room with our boxer and bulldog panting loudly, their leads wrapping around her legs in their eagerness to get to me. I cannot describe how much I had missed them; just having Molly and Barry in the same room as me lifted my spirits.

While I enjoyed being slobbered on, Lois stood at the bottom of my bed, helping with my physio.

'Pachow, pachow,' she said, as she stuck both of her middle fingers up at me and then blew the smoke off each one.

I tried to return the gesture but the middle finger on my right hand wasn't quite there. We'd been working on it for a few days, but it couldn't seem to separate itself from the rest of the pack.

'You have a face like an abandoned baboon,' she continued, pacing at the end of my bed and winding her middle finger up at me.

Again, I tried to give her the middle finger on my right hand – it was closer this time.

'Your father smells of elderberries!'

'Lois, you stole that from Monty Python.'

'So what?' she said. 'It's a great insult.'

I tried again and this time my middle finger stood up by itself. It was clawed, but it was definitely doing the job it was supposed to.

'Wooo!' Lois shouted, while clapping at the same time.

At that moment my friend, Souto, came into the room and I greeted him with my middle finger.

'That's more like it,' he said, as he returned the gesture. 'I brought you a burrito from Las Iguanas.'

'Excellent,' I responded, still holding my finger up at him. 'Lois, meet my middle finger.' I swivelled it round to her. I was so pleased with being able to do it, I couldn't help myself.

'I'm going to take the dogs out for a walk,' Lois said, smiling as she called them to her. Barry padded over to her but Molly was reluctant to leave, so Lois had to cajole her towards the door. 'I'll be back in an hour.'

Souto pulled up the chair next to me and plonked the plastic bag onto my bed.

I stared at the bag and then at him.

'Oh, shit. Sorry,' he said, remembering that I couldn't actually feed myself. My right arm had gained some movement, but I still couldn't repeatedly lift my arm all the way to my mouth.

He unwrapped the paper from the top third of the Burrito and held it close to my mouth. I took a bite.

'I had a great bank holiday weekend,' Souto said, as he held the burrito out for me again.

I took another bite. I was starving, and with a full mouth said, 'Was it a bank holiday Monday this week?'

'Yeah, first week of May, isn't it?'

I thought back to Pete coming in on Monday to start my physio. He'd come in on his day off to help me. What a legend.

Souto held out the burrito for me again. I hadn't quite swallowed the last bite but took another bite anyway.

'It's so hot in here,' Souto said, pulling at his shirt. 'I don't know how you cope with it.'

I couldn't answer him as my mouth was full of burrito. We were going through a heatwave and the hospital wasn't able to turn the heating off. So, as well as it being twenty-five degrees outside, the hot air from my large radiator continued pumping into the room. On top of this, I had a two-inch-thick foam collar around my neck connected to a plate that went halfway down my chest that couldn't be removed.

It had been so stifling last night that I hadn't been able to sleep at all. Sweat had dripped down my face and I'd managed to knock the buzzer off my bed so couldn't call the nurses to help me have a sip of water. They'd been quite surprised when they'd answered the ward telephone and heard me on the end. I'd managed to find the number on the internet and call it through my iPad – needs must.

Souto was glaring at the radiator as he held the burrito out for me again. Misjudging the distance, he smooshed it into my closed mouth as I squeaked in protest.

'Maybe if I got a wrench . . .' he said. He took the burrito away and I watched in mild horror as he took a large bite from it before smooshing it back in my face. 'That might work . . .'

I gulped down everything in my mouth. 'Souto! Stop eating my food, it's gross! And look at me when you're feeding me!'

'Oh, sorry mate. Didn't even realise.'

'You're right, though,' I said, following his gaze over to the radiator. 'I wish something could be done about the heating. I feel like my head is being roasted in here.'

'Maybe I could pop out and buy you one of those little hand-held fans. I could tie it onto the frame next to your iPad. It would cool your face and blow your hair around, like you're in a shampoo commercial.'

I grinned at him through the layer of burrito he had deposited on my face. He was a tool, but I was lucky to have him.

Nine years earlier . . .

'You'll be great, bud. Just don't fuck it up.'

Don't fuck it up. Don't fuck it up. The final words of the good luck phone call from Tom rang around my head as I entered the Recreation Ground. He and Rich, the third leg of our school friend tripod, would be there in a couple of hours to watch me play. It wasn't the fanciest of mantras, but the spirit of it was right.

Sitting on the edge of the bench in the changing room, I unnecessarily adjusted my sock again as I listened to the coaches' pre-game talk. I still couldn't get my head around how this had happened so fast. I was nineteen and about to play my first professional game of rugby. There had been a bit of an injury crisis, which meant I'd been called up early. I'd thought it would be at least another couple of years before I got this chance. Looking around me, I certainly felt on the lean side. It takes years to build up the muscle required for rugby and I was ten years younger than a lot of the other players.

The ref knocked on the door and all fifteen of us swung our heads towards the sound. It was time. Keeping my features completely still, I joined the shuffle of teammates moving towards the tunnel. Outside we met our opponents, the Leicester Tigers, who had just come out of their changing room. They were Bath's biggest rivals. I felt sick with nerves as I watched them run down the tunnel ahead of us. It wasn't the size of them that scared me; it was the pressure of messing this up. At that moment, I would have given anything for the game to be cancelled. At the same time, I knew that my dream of playing professional rugby was about to come true. All the years of training and sacrifices had narrowed and settled on a single game of eighty minutes. *Don't fuck it up.*

As I trotted after my teammates down the darkened tunnel towards the light of the stadium, I thought about all the people I knew who were watching this match. My family, friends, neighbours, Dad's colleagues, teachers . . . this was my home team and I'd lived in Bath all my life. There were probably even a few people from my primary school in the stands.

Emerging onto the pitch, I tried not to react to the roar of the crowd as we took up our positions. The noise was overwhelming as I'd never played in front of many people before. And now here I was, in front of twelve thousand.

My playing position was Number 8, which coincidentally had always been my lucky number. It's also the only position in rugby that is actually named after its number. So, I had told myself this must be doubly lucky, and I needed all the luck I could get.

Playing Number 8 meant that I had been tasked with the first important action of the game, catching the kick off. It was really helping my anxiety levels to know that all eyes in the stadium would be drilling down on to me, judging me on this one make-or-break moment.

Dontfuckitup, dontfuckitup, dontfuckitup. The mantra sped up as I waited for the ref's whistle. Despite what was whirring through my mind, I kept my face completely still. I was desperate not to reveal what I was feeling.

The whistle blew and sure enough the kicker shaped to send the ball my way. The thump of leather connecting with the ball was the only sound I could hear as everything went into slow motion. I tracked the ball, high above the line of the stands. I was very aware of the eight pumped-up Leicester forwards at full tilt, hoping to knock me into next week as soon as I caught it . . . if I caught it.

Before I knew it, I found myself at the bottom of a pile of players, but importantly with the ball in my hands. I had caught it. The nerves immediately fell away. It was game on . . .

With only twenty minutes until the end of the match, I could honestly say I'd done pretty well. Sixty minutes of hard physical work had made getting quickly off the ground more difficult. When I next pulled myself up, my attention was drawn to Alesana Tuilagi who was heading straight for me. Nineteen stone of pure muscle and one of the most powerful players in the Premiership. He stared straight at me as he quickened his pace. I turned towards him, braced myself for the impact and drove into his legs.

I opened my eyes. All I could see was the grey, tumultuous sky.

The edges of my vision were hazy, and my head rang, blocking out all other noise.

'Ed.' A woman's voice broke through. 'Can you hear me?'

'Hummm,' was all I could manage.

'I don't want you to move. Don't even nod.'

'I'm 'kay . . .'

'You might think you're okay, but you gave us a scare. You've been out for a while.'

I blinked rapidly to try and clear my vision. It was only then that I realised that I was lying in the middle of the rugby pitch with twelve thousand people staring down at me.

'Can you move your left hand,' a man said.

I squeezed it around his fingers.

'What about your right hand?'

I gave that one a squeeze too.

Remembering my dad, I imagined him standing up in his seat,

peering down at me. He would be worrying about whether I was still unconscious. He wouldn't be able to see from that far away that I was awake and following the doctor's instructions not to move. Christ, he'll be worried, I thought.

'And push down on my hand with the other foot.'

I followed his instructions, desperate to get up so I could show Dad that I was okay.

'All right, it seems there was no damage,' he concluded. 'But that's you done for the day.'

The doctor and the physio offered me their hands to help me stand. The crowd clapped as I wobbled to my feet. I tried to smile and wave at them as I made my way over to the entranceway of the tunnel.

You fucked it up . . .

I was devastated; it had hardly been the dream start.

The following Monday, I sat quietly as I waited for the defence coach to meet with me. That morning, I'd dressed as smartly as my rugby kit would allow and tried to plaster down my unruly hair. I wanted to look my best when I received my P45; I thought it might help when my pride took a battering. As I waited outside the coach's office, I wondered if this was the shortest rugby career in history. No, there must have been someone who'd messed things up in the first half of their opening match. It didn't make me feel any better.

'Come in, Ed,' the defence coach said, opening his office door.

I followed him inside and took a seat opposite.

'I need to talk to you about Saturday.'

I nodded, unable to form any words.

'I've got the recording so we can watch it over together.'

Great, my humiliation would be complete.

I watched in silence as the figure on the screen braced for Tuilagi. It wasn't pretty.

'I've also got a few other clips for you to watch as well.'

He pressed another button and I watched three other matches, clearly taken at different times and places. Each one featured Tuilagi.

'He regularly does this,' the coach said.

We carried on watching the matches. In each clip he showed me, whomever Tuilagi charged at effectively got out of his way.

'What matters,' the coach continued, 'is that you tried. You stuck your head in when lots of other players shy away.'

'So, I'm not fired then?' I asked.

The coach gave me a broad smile. 'No. Not this time.'

As I lay in my dark overheated hospital room, I thought back to that first rugby match. At that moment, back when I was nineteen, something had clicked into place for me and from then on I'd hung my hat on effort. At every club I played for, I made sure that I wasn't going to let anyone question my effort. I'm not saying I was the best, but I made sure that I was one of the fittest because it was something I had control over. I worked hard to achieve that target. Because no matter how bad the task made me feel at the time, if it resulted in any sort of progress, then it was worth it.

That's the thing about motivation, it won't often present itself to you, ready for you to grasp. If you sit around waiting for it, it becomes a shy creature, often out of reach. One of the few certainties in life is that time will pass. You can spend the next hour doing something that will make a difference. Or you can spend it waiting for motivation to show its face. Either way, an hour will pass. Best use it wisely.

The next morning, I was ready to go. Effort was what I'd hung my hat on before and it was what would get me through this time as well.

Pete and Wyn had visited me first thing and Pete had begun to test if there was any movement in my left leg. He would hold my foot in his hand and push the leg up, so my knee bent and thigh moved towards my chest.

'I can definitely feel a twitch in your left leg,' Pete said.

I couldn't feel a thing. Pete had said this a few times and I was beginning to wonder whether he was saying this to encourage me or if it was really there.

'Ooh, there was another one.'

'Hmm . . .' I responded.

Don't get me wrong, Pete was highly skilled at what he did. After years of experience he had turned physio into an art form; it was beyond a science for him. He had a gift and a way of feeling his way across a body that was almost instinctive. But perhaps his encouraging words weren't a true reflection of my physical state.

As we took a break, I showed Pete some of the movement coming back in my left arm. I couldn't move my hand at all, but coupled with the movement in my right arm that had been increasing over the last couple of weeks, I was getting close to being able to bench press. When I say bench press, I hope you include a 20cm lift with my right arm holding a rolled-up magazine. My biggest problem was grip. My left hand hung limply and refused to support anything.

After inspecting my arm, Pete tried putting a broom handle in both of my hands. I could loosely curl my right hand around it, but my left one just flapped around. He extended my left wrist and I watched as my left hand clawed around the broom handle.

'Don't get excited,' Pete warned. 'It's just a tenodesis grasp, an automatic reaction, not the real thing.'

Still, with my hand clawed around the broom handle, it meant I could balance it and begin my small bench presses. The idea of being able to do an actual bench press, however small, by myself – my own exercise regime – was enough to give me a small spark of hope.

Next up was the tilt table. If you ever saw a tilt table out of context, you'd be forgiven for thinking that it was some sort of medieval torture device. The theory to it is simple. Apart from my recent visits to the grandad chair, I'd been on my back for a month and even sitting up would sometimes make me feel dizzy. The accident had affected some of my automatic responses as well as my motor and sensory function. So, before I could even consider being back on my feet, my body had to be trained to regulate its own blood pressure again.

Lie down on a table, stay still, get tilted forwards. Sounds simple enough, but Pete had warned me that the tilt table could double up as a good way to get information out of people. Over the next hour, Pete increased the gradient of the table until my blood pressure dropped. He would then bring me back down again until it normalised. This process was then repeated until I tried to punch him or pass out.

The further up it went, the harder the adjustment. On the eighth trip I could feel my right hand automatically grasp for anything to try to steady myself.

'Are you all right?' Pete asked from the side of the table.

'Umhum,' was all I could manage.

The world was closing in on me and my body had gone into panic mode trying to protect me from unseen dangers. As the blood drained from my head all I could feel was an impending sense of doom. The warnings now all made sense. Although safe, the repetitive nature of the process resembled entry-level torture. As horrific as it was, I was still enjoying pushing myself to the edge again.

Pete lowered me down and my body began to settle. I counted out two minutes in my head.

Testing myself physically is what I've always enjoyed. Always have, always will. My first rugby match had taught me that there is no progression unless you are pushed out of your comfort zone. When I stripped it back, I realised that was all this situation was, another test of endurance. The stakes may have been higher, but the rules hadn't changed.

When I'd finished counting the minutes in my head, I looked at Pete directly. 'I'm ready. Take me up again.'

It was early evening and Lois was sitting on the edge of my bed. The other visitors had trailed away for their evening plans and for once it was just the two of us. Lois was quieter that evening and I suspected that she had something to tell me. Some of my dad's friends had visited and offered me tickets to see Fleetwood Mac in August . . . in New York. They knew it was unlikely I would make it, but it gave me something to aim for, something that maybe I could do. In the end, I asked her what was worrying her.

'It's the wedding,' she replied. 'I know it's unlikely you'll make it to New York and it's a lovely motivator for you, but we have to think realistically about the wedding next year. The next instalment is due to be paid and we can't afford to lose the money. I think we both know it's not going to happen, so we shouldn't keep on paying money towards it.'

I tried to meet her gaze. I knew she was right. An image flashed into my mind of me lying on a hospital bed under the arched flowers, unable to even appreciate the view of the Tuscan hills. We'd chosen the venue of our dreams, but it just wasn't practical, or even possible, to travel to Italy.

'I'm sorry, Lois. I know how much you were looking forward to it.'

'It is what it is,' she said. 'We can try again the following year maybe.'

I smiled at her. 'Give me your hand.'

She slipped her hand with the engagement ring she always wore into my palm.

I gave it the gentlest squeeze.

That night, after typing out another Instagram post, I lay in my hospital bed staring up at the ceiling. I had posted every single day that week but hadn't wanted to check the responses. It was hard enough opening up about what was happening to me, without also finding out what people thought of it.

The nurses had told Lois she could stay for the night. She was curled up on the floor next to me on an air bed. I didn't know whether she was asleep yet; probably not. She would be thinking about how different our year had turned out.

I had let her down. She had been counting down the days to this wedding. The man she intended to marry had been taken away from her and now she couldn't even have the day she wanted. I had to make it up to her somehow. I knew nothing would replace the day we had been looking forward to. But there must be something I could do for her . . . then it came to me.

'Lois, are you still awake?'

'Yes.' There was a rasping sound to her voice that I didn't recognise. 'Do you need some water?'

'No, I'm fine. I've been thinking, you should still go on the netball tour around New Zealand this summer.'

'Don't be daft, Ed,' Lois mumbled. 'I can't do that. I'd be gone for two weeks.'

'You can and you should. I've got my physio to concentrate on—'

'Two hours a day isn't going to keep you occupied.'

'The lads have said they'll be my replacement Pete when he's not around. I won't have a spare minute.'

A small, white lie. There was only so much physio my friends could do without access to the right equipment, but I knew it would help.

There was the unmistakable sound of Lois clambering out of her sleeping bag and a second later she was sitting on my bed.

'Are you sure? No, don't say it now. Have a think about it. You can sleep on it. We'll talk about it tomorrow.'

I smiled at her in the dark as I took her hand. I wouldn't be changing my mind. This road to recovery wasn't just about my physical state; it was about everyone around me returning to their lives as well.

CHAPTER 7

SECOND TIME FOR FIRSTS

It was a Friday morning, a month after my accident, and I'd had my two hours of physio for the day. It would be another three days before I'd get to do anything with Pete and Wynn again. I was ready to do three whole days, put the effort in, but there was no one available to do it with me. Pete had all the other patients on the ward to see and the hospital closed down at weekends.

If Pete had a catch phrase, it would be 'ramp it up'. I concluded that because I was hearing him utter these words more often, it was a sign that we were making progress. Naturally, as I became stronger, I was able to handle more and this was exactly what I needed.

In the last two days I'd seen a flicker of life in my left hand. My left side was swinging back into action and I could now bench press my broom handle by 30cm. The question now was, did the NHS have the resources to provide the necessary hours of rehab that I needed?

Restart, a charity that supports professional rugby players, had told me and my family that they would help us get the best care possible. I was incredibly grateful to them for their generous offer but knew that they couldn't begin organising this for me until I was discharged from hospital. While an inpatient, I wasn't allowed to mix private physio with NHS physio for insurance reasons. I was still waiting for a place to open up at an NHS specialist spinal unit but I'd been told that this could take weeks, even months.

My enthusiasm threatened to ebb and frustration had started to creep back in. Previously, I'd coped with frustration by focusing on the process, not the outcome. But this was a different situation. I didn't have access to the hours of physio that I needed, so I couldn't focus on the process.

At night, I had tortured myself by reading up on spinal cord treatment in America and Japan. I knew the NHS was years behind in providing what had become standardised in other countries. It was overstretched and underfunded. All the studies I'd read showed that volume and early intervention could make the difference between walking and a wheelchair.

I'd also looked up the cost of a private spinal rehab hospital as well. I had to check it twice as I couldn't believe it – ten thousand pounds a week. Ten thousand pounds a week! That amount of money was insane . . . But then at night, when I was alone and terrified of being a burden to Lois or my mum for the rest of my life, I began to wonder. How much would I pay to walk again? What if I missed the chance to become independent? With the gift of hindsight, would a future me be wishing that I'd paid for private treatment now? I could sell my house in Cardiff; that would give me a few months . . .

As I churned over the options, I'd tried to come up with innovative ways of carrying on my physio while Pete wasn't there. I would use anything around me with a bit of weight to it and strap it to my wrist and try to lift it. Movement was creeping down from my shoulders to my hands. Pete would pop into my room between seeing patients and plonk the broom handle into my right hand and say, 'Give me four hundred reps.' Pete's military background mixed with my career as a professional sportsperson meant his methods resonated well with me. I would usually get competitive, so by the time he came back, 400 reps had often turned into 600.

I'd recently persuaded some rugby player mates to take off the hollow, metal footplate at the bottom of my bed and wrap my curled hands around it. I then used this as my new weight to bench press as it was a couple of kilos heavier. A few times it had slipped out of my hands and clonked me on the nose, resulting in a nosebleed, but I didn't mind.

As I worked my way through another set of reps while chatting to Lois, Rich and my brother Josh, I was pleased to see two of the nurses pop their heads around my door.

'We thought we'd come and have lunch with you.'

'You two again?' I said, smiling at them. 'We've got Lois's current favourite, *13 Reasons Why*, on. Come on in and talk loudly over it if you want. The louder, the better.'

'Oooh, I haven't seen this one,' the taller nurse said, taking one of the spare seats.

They both settled down and we all chatted as we half paid attention to the programme.

'What have you got for lunch?' I asked, peering towards their lunch boxes.

'Ed,' Lois said, 'you only ate an hour ago.' She turned to the nurses. 'Ignore him, he's already had three meals today. He's pretty far from being starved.'

'Here, you can have this,' one of the nurses said, popping a mini Babybel into my mouth. 'In exchange, I want some of your belly button fluff so I can sell it on eBay and retire.'

'Think you better lower your expectations on how much that would raise,' I responded.

'Not now that you're famous,' Rich teased. 'Haven't you checked your Instagram account?'

'No. I've been posting but haven't looked at the responses.'

'You should take a look,' Lois said. 'Things have started taking off.'

'Oh yeah?' I said, as I continued with my broom handle reps. 'I'll have a look tonight.'

A phone was dangled in front of my nose and the broom handle was taken out of my hands.

'Take a look now,' Lois said.

My Instagram account took up the screen. She pointed at the corner.

'Oh,' I said, hardly believing what I was seeing. 'Ten thousand is quite a lot. Isn't it?'

In the space of a week I had gained ten thousand followers. I switched on my iPad and began scrolling through all the messages.

The following day was my stepbrother's birthday and, after a meal out, the whole family and several of his friends were coming to visit me to round off the celebrations. Sixteen of us in total would be packed into my new room. I'd recently had an upgrade and was now the grateful owner of a side room with an en suite. It didn't get much better than that on Helena Ward. Having an en suite also meant that for the first time since the accident, I could have a shower.

Sometimes, I would lie still in my hospital bed and pretend

there was nothing wrong with me. I was just lying in a normal bed, waiting for an excuse to get up. I'd imagine that I'd got home from a ten-kilometre run with Lois and we'd both crashed out for a mid-afternoon nap. Or, I would take us away on holiday. We were jet-lagged, having woken up at 3 a.m., discussing whether to get up and watch the sunrise together. It was a game I would play that helped me to relax. It offered me a bit of peace now and again.

The opposite to this was being stripped naked, transferred in a hoist to a chair and wheeled into a bathroom to be washed down by two people I had only just met.

I had never felt so disabled as I did the moment I was hoisted, naked, out of bed. I was tucked up and winched over my bed, my body balled up tight with the bottom half of my legs and arms spraying out in different directions. Even if I could move, I would never have been able to get out of this contraption. I felt incredibly vulnerable.

What if this is the end of my recovery? Will Lois or my mum have to learn how to do this?

I'd never given much thought to the process of getting out of bed. It was just something I did while thinking about what I was going to do later that day. Now it took twenty minutes and a team of three people. For all my 30cm bench presses and flickering left hand, I was still incredibly far from where I wanted to be.

Sitting on the special plastic chair under the shower, it was lovely to feel the water run down my back and to have my hair washed. Perhaps it would have been more pleasant if there weren't two people I hadn't met before staring at me. The process did have an upside, though. Running the shower over me showed that although I couldn't differentiate between hot and cold on my right side, my left side was progressing and starting to feel more normal.

I'm sure that, after four weeks, everyone else was very excited that I was finally getting to have a shower, but it was one of the worst experiences I had in hospital. Lying in a bed you can forget; you can kid yourself that you're in a beach hut in Bali. Having a shower stripped away all those fantasies and shone a cold, hard light on the reality of my situation. It also gave me a glimpse at what the rest of my life could be.

There was a mirror on the back of the door in the bathroom. As I was hoisted from the shower seat, I forced myself to take a long look at my body. I could definitely see that the muscles wastage had begun to do its worst. The thick strips of muscle around my neck had gone, my chest had shrunk, as had my legs. I suppose I still had more muscle than most people, but that wasn't the point. I didn't look like me anymore and that hurt. The worst thing was that I knew there was more wastage to come. It wouldn't just stop today because I'd finally seen myself. It's not easy watching the person you know disappearing by the day.

After my shower I had my first haircut since the accident, and I was weighed. Back in bed again, clean as a whistle and with a new lid, I thought about the two and a half stone I'd lost. All I'd had to do was lie down and do nothing for a month. Some people may think, 'Perfect, summer's coming. I'll just tuck myself up in bed for the run up to Ibiza', but that's the thing: none of my weight loss was fat. It was all muscle. Ten years' worth of muscle that I'd worked hard every day to build and maintain. At fifteen stone, I was the lightest I'd been since I was 14 years old.

If I said that watching my body change didn't bother

me, I would be lying. Of course it did. But if I let myself dwell on this, let it affect me, then I would be wasting time instead of concentrating on what was important.

I knew I had to stop myself worrying about things I couldn't affect or control. I had wasted so much energy wondering where I would be in a year. Or re-running the accident and what I could have done to stop myself from diving into the pool. Instead, I should have used this energy positively and worked harder on my rehab. Only try to control the controllable.

'I have an ideal,' Pete said, in his West Country accent.

'What's your idea?' I asked, intrigued.

'My ideal is that if we prop you up on the tilt table in the hallway, I can check on you between seeing other patients.'

I grinned. More time on the tilt table meant more time in rehab. I was up for it.

'I'm also going to apply to the board for more physio time for you,' Pete said, while continuing to press into my legs.

The spasms were at their most prolific in the mornings. A yawn and a stretch would often spark a wave of tension to run from my back into my legs, followed with some vibrating for a few seconds. As my right leg improved, the spasms became less frequent. In fact, they were almost entirely favouring the weaker left side. The spasms weren't painful; they would sometimes prove quite pleasant as they provided a brief respite to the mundane stillness of my left leg.

A strange thing had started to happen: I had begun to control the spasms. By tensing my stomach and shifting my weight a little, I could send a spasm rolling down my body. Although not strictly under my control, it was such a relief to feel those dormant muscles kick back into life.

Pete was pressing down on my left leg and muttering his usual encouraging words, which sometimes sounded like incantations. Not having any sensory feedback in terms of movement or joint position was a difficult hurdle to overcome and my faith in the truth of his words was constantly being tested.

Pete pushed down again. Then something happened.

I felt something fire up in my left quad. Something bloody well fired in my passenger leg! A huge wave of excitement rolled over me, followed immediately by a sobering nervousness. Was that real? Or was it just another spasm?

'I told you so,' Pete said, raising an eyebrow. 'Let's do a retest.'

He pushed down again.

I felt it. A twitch that told me that my left leg was back in the game.

I had always hoped that I would walk again. I had always tried to stay positive. But at that moment, I knew there was a real chance it could happen.

Excited to share my news, I called my family and friends for an impromptu party in my room that evening. For me, the celebrations were limited to cranberry juice and a laxative. But a win's a win.

We had friends round for lunch; I could hear their laughter from the kitchen as Lois loaded me up with plates of food to take out to them.

'Can you manage?' she asked, after kissing me lightly on the cheek.

'Of course!' I said, giving her one of my most winning smiles as I balanced the tray laden with food.

I turned from her and walked into the garden. It was hot and I blinked against the sudden brightness of the sunlight. Our friends turned to me expectantly and, sensing that the moment required a touch of showmanship, I did a little two-step dance before putting the tray of food on the table . . .

I woke up with a light sheen of sweat over my body. For a moment I thought I could still walk again and I was still that man who could carry a plate of food out to his friends. It took a few minutes to realise where I was. And that I wasn't that man anymore.

Paul, the gentleman who cleaned my room every day, was emptying my bin. It had been another brutal night of being unable to cough for an hour and barely being able to sleep until 3 a.m.

Paul glanced over to me as he put a new liner into my bin. 'You been having the dreams again?'

'Is it that obvious?'

'I reckon I'd have the same if I was in your place. I imagine it's normal. They'll change as you get used to it.'

'I could ask some of the other patients I've made contact with about it,' I said, while considering the possibility.

Paul straightened up. 'I think that's a good idea. You'll be full of them today if you've already had one by this time in the morning.'

I smiled at him; perhaps I would have a few breakthroughs today.

I hadn't told anyone about the dreams. I didn't want to burden my family or friends with them. Paul was my only confidante when it came to my night-time worries and that was simply because he had witnessed me waking up from them.

I'd received lots of messages of support from people through Instagram: some had just been diagnosed with a spinal injury themselves; others were a few months or years down the line. The majority were well-wishers who had said that they'd been inspired by my positive reaction to the accident and it had helped put their own worries into perspective. It felt as if, finally, something positive was coming out of my accident. There had been a shift inside of me and it had made way for something new. I had begun to understand the power of helping yourself by helping others.

I knew it was time to reach out to the people who were further down the line and see what might be waiting for me. There were some things I just couldn't tell my family (or Paul for that matter). I needed to speak to someone who understood what I had been through.

Paul carried on cleaning my room and we chatted away as we always did. As he left, I had a thought. I hoped that the cleaners and healthcare assistants all knew how important they were to the patients. The first person a patient sees in the morning has a huge impact on their day. Not everyone gets to be a Mr Barua and save a spine with tweezers and a microscope, but we could all try to be a Paul and turn someone's recovery around.

The last couple of days had revolved around building on the power that was returning in my left leg. My blood pressure was finally starting to behave itself and now the second major benefit of the tilt table was becoming apparent. The nervous system is most active when upright, and working on the tilt table was allowing me to put pressure through the seven thousand nerve endings in each of my feet. My left leg was still feeling very strange. Nothing was firing below the knee and I wasn't receiving much feedback, but the power was improving. Things had started moving along quickly. We kept pushing, kept ticking things off and driving on.

One morning Pete bounded into my room and I knew just by looking at him that he had something up his sleeve.

'I've been looking at your progress and me and Wyn think you're ready,' he announced.

'For . . .' I responded.

'To stand, of course,' he said, looking at me as if I had missed the whole point of physio over the past few weeks.

Fortunately, he didn't expect me to do this by myself and instead introduced me to a new piece of equipment. It was like a very tall, static Zimmer frame. As I held on to its two joysticks, Pete fitted the braces around my knees.

'Are you ready?' he asked as he stood by the controls.

I nodded.

Slowly I was winched up by the large strap he had already secured around my back.

'Now's the difficult bit,' Pete said.

Using my back and elbows, I tried to pull myself upwards and do as much of the standing as possible, with the machine taking care of the rest. It took me straight back to the first time I tried to sit up. My muscles ached and threatened to tip me over in every direction. I quickly realised that the challenge was getting my balance – it always came back to those core muscles.

Ten attempts and a few spasms later, I was up. When I was fully straight, I took a moment to enjoy it. For the first time in weeks, I was standing on my own two feet. My left leg still felt like a prosthetic and I was wobbling around like I'd had one too many pints, but my God it felt good to be back on my feet.

Four days ago, a flicker in my left leg, and now, with help, I was standing.

I made a decision right then. Instead of looking at what I'd lost for the first time because of the accident, I was going to concentrate on what I'd gained for the second time during my recovery.

Later that day, Pete delivered the news that the board had approved his request and I would be able to get extra hours of physio with him. Relief flooded through me – I didn't need to consider changing hospital anymore. Was there somewhere with better equipment? Probably. Was there somewhere with more physios? Most likely. Was there somewhere with funnier nurses? I doubt it. Was there somewhere with another Pete? Definitely not.

Yes, my room was unbearably hot and perhaps in a private hospital there would be air conditioning. But Helena Ward went above and beyond in every respect. They were like one large family who knew they didn't have the fanciest equipment or the most cutting-edge procedures, but they improvised and made up for it in other ways.

Because that's the thing: recovery isn't just about the standard of equipment or the hours they could put in. It's about good mental health as well. Without that standard baseline, my motivation would have slipped. Without motivation, I would have still been lying in my bed, worrying about my recovery, or drifting away and living in the past.

Don't judge a hospital by its cover. It's not always the millions of pounds of equipment that matters; it's the people.

CHAPTER 8

ROLL WITH IT (BUT NOT ALL THE TIME)

'A place has opened up for you at Salisbury Spinal Unit. You'll be leaving Bath tomorrow,' Pete informed me.

My face fell.

At the beginning of my stay at Bath hospital I had fantasised about hearing those words more than once. But the progress I had made on Helena Ward showed that my current rehab was working for me, and it was working well. The old adage, 'If it ain't broke, don't fix it', sprang to mind. I realised that was a ridiculous thing to think, considering I was broken and would quite like to be fixed. However, I'd been on a tilt table most of that morning and the progress with my makeshift bench press had brought even more movement to both of my arms. When I'd arrived in Helena Ward, I'd still been on bed rest, with only a few twitching fingers and toes. Pete, Wyn and I had hit a groove; we understood each other now. Pete would set the boundaries but also let me cautiously test them.

'And I have to go?' I asked.

I was sitting up in my grandad chair, minus the peddles and monitor, where I'd spent most of my days.

'I'm afraid so,' Pete said, shuffling his notes around and not quite meeting my eye. 'Once a space opens you are expected to leave this hospital. There are a few things I have to tell you about the specialist spinal units. Well prepared is well armed and all that.'

I looked up at him, ready to take on any advice he had to give me.

'You'll have more access to physio and different types of rehab there,' Pete began. 'There will be different therapists who can start helping you relearn all the things the body needs in order to become independent again. They have loads of equipment, and things like a hydrotherapy pool, which you haven't used before. But when you get there, they'll put you back on bed rest. They'll want to assess you for themselves and won't rely on our findings. So, you'll have to jump through a few hoops before you can start your rehab again.'

I took a moment to think about it. 'So, I won't be able to practise standing for a while?'

Pete nodded. 'It's why I've been pushing for you to stand before you leave here. I knew you'd be transferred soon, and, if you can stand, it means that they are bound by the protocols to work towards you walking. If we just had you sitting, then they'd aim to discharge you in a wheelchair.'

I'd always known a large part of my past recovery was down to Pete. Now, he was taking care of my future recovery too.

I looked at Pete with new respect. 'Why didn't you say anything? I didn't know you'd done this for me.'

He began to check the hoist next to my bed. 'I didn't want to get your hopes up and then crush them if I couldn't get you standing. You didn't need that pressure, what with everything else.'

'Thank you,' I said, hoping those two words would convey everything I was feeling.

'It's all right,' Pete said, finally meeting my eye. 'I knew we had a chance with you as you're motivated to get better.'

'Well, if I'm leaving tomorrow, there's one more thing I'd like to do.'

An hour later, I was still in my wheelie grandad chair, but it was parked up in a different place. The back had been lowered and the footrest had been pushed up. The urine bag for my catheter was hanging off the side. If a hospital bed and a La-Z-Boy reclining chair had a summer fling, this might have been the outcome. It was another hot day and I closed my eyes, letting the sunlight smooth out the tension that had begun to surface on my skin in the recent weeks.

Pete was sitting in one of the lightweight visitors chairs next to me, his legs stretched out and his Armani sunglasses on. Molly was lying between my legs, enjoying a bit of al fresco time with me. Occasionally, I could hear the birds' calls above the low rumble of cars reversing in and out of the parking spaces. It wasn't a bad way to end my stay in Helena Ward. And if it happened that the only free space to park my chair in the hospital car park was one of the consultants', then I was taking it.

The next morning, before leaving for Salisbury, my six closest female friends from school piled into my room. A few of them had brought their babies and all of them had something tasty to eat. Five of them were sitting on my bed, everyone was talking at once, one of the toddlers was circling the room pulling a balloon, and I had the other sleeping baby propped into the crook of my arm.

All too soon they were wishing me good luck as the paramedics came to collect me for my transfer to a new hospital. I'd already said my individual goodbyes to the staff and I'd put up a post on Instagram that summarised my feelings on leaving:

I am coming away from the RUH with about six adopted mums, two brothers, twelve Filipino cousins and a Godfather so it's been a busy month. Mandy, thanks for threatening to clip each one of my mates around the ear. Lorraine, I'll keep hold of that belly button fluff (don't ask). Sharon, I won't say what you said, and Andy, don't have too much fun in Thailand. Pete, Wyn, you know what you've done already, I'm not going to thank you yet because we're not done! . . . I'll miss all you bonkers lot but I'll be back in as soon as I get home, behave yourselves.

Looking around at the lilac walls of the ward that I had initially dismissed as the wrong place for my recovery, I hoped that the next stage of my journey would be just as successful.

The ambulance rumbled along the country roads that connected Bath to Salisbury. I was half listening to the ambulance driver's *The Best of Faces* album, which he had already played through twice. My mind drifted and I began to imagine what I would be doing if the accident hadn't have happened. Now that I was spending more time on social media, I was more aware of what other people were getting up to. I couldn't help but make comparisons with my own life. That's the downside to those carefully filtered snippets of other peoples' lives – it makes our thoughts automatically jump to our own reality.

It was officially holiday season for rugby players and around now Lois and I would have been packing our bags for a trip away. My friends' holiday pictures were starting to pop up on my Instagram feed and I was beginning to suffer from a very severe case of FOMO. Don't get me wrong, I was happy for my friends that were getting a bit of early summer sunshine – they'd worked hard all year and deserved it. But it would've been nice if I could be out there with them, with Lois, who needed a holiday more than ever. The negative thoughts popped into my head, one after the other, dragging me down with them.

I knew I had to do something to stop this spiral, so I started reframing those thoughts. This is a technique I've mentioned before and maybe one you've heard of. For those of you who haven't come across this little gem of a mind hack, then I'm going to go into a bit more detail here now.

We all have an inner monologue that can either be our most vehement champion or harshest critic. Reframing thoughts is a way of turning critical or negative thoughts into positive ones.

'I can't believe that diving into a pool left me with only 4mm of spinal cord' became, 'At least I have 4mm of spinal cord left; it gives me the chance of a recovery.'

'I feel bad that all my friends, family and Lois have to spend all their free time with me. I'm sure there are other places they'd rather be' became, 'I'm lucky to have friends and family who want to visit me. I'm lucky to have Lois.'

'If I have to listen to *The Best of Faces* album for a third time, I might release the brake on my bed and see where the open road takes me' became, 'At least I'm relaxed enough to be able to listen to the music. The last ambulance journey I was worrying about damaging my spine the entire time.'

So what if I couldn't go on holiday this year? There would be other holidays in the future, even if I didn't make any further recovery. Reframing leads to rethinking. And rethinking leads to re-feeling.

As I arrived at Salisbury spinal unit, a modern hospital with a triangular, peaked roof, I prepared myself to meet a whole new group of people. Not only would I have to go through the usual routine of meeting new staff members – 'Hello, I'm Ed. Yes, we can do a manual evacuation now if you want . . .' – but I'd soon be meeting all of the other patients as well. I'd been in my own bubble at the previous hospitals and now I would be on one of the open wards with eight other patients.

I was rolled into a side room and informed by the nurse that I would be in a private room for two days as they carried out the checks and assessments Pete had told me about. He'd been right that the new team wanted to form their own opinion of my condition.

Mum and Lois began unloading all of my paraphernalia and Dad was on hand for when I met the consultant. I remained lying down in my hospital bed, even though I'd spent most of my time sitting up for the last couple of weeks. There were new rules to abide by.

It clearly wasn't the hospital's first rodeo. In the space of four hours, I'd had three X-rays, two ultrasounds, an ASIA test, been measured for a wheelchair, and met the consultant. I'd made her jump when I'd pulled my right arm out to shake her hand. She'd only seen my original scans so had presumed that I was a complete spinal cord injury with no movement below the neck. She'd actually jumped. I knew then that they hadn't read my notes, and if they had, they were still going to treat me as if my accident was yesterday.

They were certainly efficient, but with efficiency came rules. I understood their reasons for being cautious; they had to protect themselves from being blamed if anything went wrong and they wanted to assess my limitations for themselves. They had made it very clear that *they* were the specialists in spinal injuries. But it was still frustrating as I was going from sitting up in a chair all day to three-hour checks for pressure sores again, which I hadn't had for weeks. This meant that every three hours during the night and day I would be woken, rolled, inspected and repositioned. It felt like a huge step backwards.

Despite my reservations, I was hopeful that I would fit in at the hospital. There was a welcoming, community feel on the wards that increased my confidence in the place. That afternoon, they were having a barbecue in the garden and although I was unable to attend in my bed, I was very kindly brought a burger, sausage bap and a Cornetto. It looked like I would be back to eighteen stone before I knew it.

After a night of being rolled around like a dinghy too far out at sea, I woke up grumpier than usual through lack of sleep. I tried to wait patiently for someone to begin my rehab, but by 3 p.m. I was still in bed. Lois had tried her best to keep me entertained, but I couldn't help but feel stuck in limbo. I wasn't being impatient; I knew that high amounts of regular rehab were essential when recovering from a spinal injury. I had been reframing my thoughts, but sometimes action needs to be taken to rectify a situation. I'm not an annoying person, at least I don't think I am, but I came to the conclusion that if I asked every half an hour to get out of bed, someone might get pissed off enough to listen.

Just as I was about to start singing loudly and out of tune, there was a knock on the door and one of the staff entered pushing a wheelchair. She positioned it at the side of my bed. We began our polite introductions, but soon she got down to business.

'So, we have to be very careful about pressure sores. I know it might be frustrating, as I understand you were sitting up a lot in your last hospital, but we have to check for them ourselves. There are procedures we have to follow.'

I nodded, waiting to hear when I could get going.

'Once you're able to get into the wheelchair, you'll have half an hour in it and then we'll check you for sores. The next day an hour, the following day an hour and a half . . .'

My eyes glazed over as I totted up the number of days it would take to reach the required four hours in a wheelchair to begin physio. Eight days!

Her voice cut back in. 'Have you done a wheelchair transfer before? If you haven't, we can spend a couple of days teaching you.'

Ten days!

'Umm, yes. Yes, I have,' I said, glancing over to Lois who was standing behind the nurse, frowning at me.

How hard can this wheelchair stuff really be?

My grandad chair back at Bath had wheels, so it was practically a wheelchair. I didn't think I'd mention that I had to be hoisted into that . . .

'Do you want to show us, then?' the nurse continued, positioning the wheelchair so it was next to my bed.

'Right. Yes. Yes, I will . . . show you.'

She helped me to the edge of the bed, and I eyed up the wheelchair. I glanced over to Lois. Her eyes were wide, but she was still my ally as she'd kept shtum.

Staring at the wheelchair, I could feel the seconds ticking by. I'd just have to go for it.

Without further ado, I launched myself at it. My backside was leading the way, flying through the air from the bed to the wheelchair. I tried to twist my body, and squeezed my eyes shut as one and a half cheeks found the canvas seat.

The nurse frowned.

'It was a bit of a dodgy one,' I said hastily, shuffling the other half a cheek into the seat before she could put me back in my bed. 'It was the pressure of being watched . . .'

She smiled. 'Well, perhaps we can go over your technique again another time.'

'Yes, yes. Thank you,' I responded. 'Lois, do you fancy wheeling me out so we can take a look at the facilities?'

Lois was around the nurse in a flash, and we both waved goodbye.

'Be back in half an hour,' the nurse called after us.

'Bloody hell, Ed,' Lois said, as she pushed me down the corridor, 'a two-legged goat could have done that with more grace.'

'Needs must, Lois.'

When we were a bit further away from the bustle of the main wards, Lois let go and I decided to have a go at driving my new set of wheels. It was surprisingly easier than I had expected. My arms had gained enough strength in the last two weeks to push at the wheels, but both my hands were curled so my fingers rubbed on the tires.

For the first time in nearly six weeks, I had my first taste of independence – I could choose in which direction I wanted to travel and when. It sounds pretty basic, but take it away and you'll quickly miss it. We started with a lap around the gardens and I found myself stopping my wheelchair so that I could watch the bees gliding between the flowers. Lois waited patiently as I wheeled towards the sound of running water. One of the courtyards had a water feature that ran around its edge and I pushed my chair towards it. Within ten minutes, my whole outlook on the place had changed. I breathed in deeply as I surveyed the wide pathway that circled the gardens and idly wondered what the lap record of the outside path of the garden was.

It's amazing what a bit a fresh air and some freedom can do. But at the back of my head there was a small thought. *I can't believe that I'm the person who needs a wheelchair* . . .

I wheeled myself back inside and headed to the far end of the building and into an empty gymnasium. Lois patiently followed, obviously aware that I'd missed the freedom of being able to roam. I parked my wheelchair up behind some exercise bars and Lois sat down on the floor next to me. I think she knew something was up, but she also knew this was important to me.

Four hours later, I took the brakes off my wheelchair and headed back to the ward. Wheeling myself back into my room, it wasn't long before one of the nurses came in.

I made sure I spoke before she had the chance. 'I'm sorry. I know it's been longer than half an hour and I will take full responsibility if there are any signs of pressure sores. But take a look and I'm one hundred per cent sure you won't find any. I was sitting up for eight hours a day in the last hospital and didn't get any.'

'We'll take a look first,' she said.

She helped me transfer back onto the bed and gave me a thorough inspection.

'You're right, there's no sign of them,' she said, peeling her gloves off. 'I can mark you down as fine to start physio.'

I gave her a broad grin and she returned my smile, humming as she sorted out the necessary paperwork.

Needs must.

CHAPTER 9

ROUGH WITH THE SMOOTH

By 10 a.m. the following morning, I realised that I'd drawn the short straw. I was at the end of the list of patients waiting for their morning routine to begin. Without a nurse to help me transfer to the toilet and shower, I couldn't get going with my day and was still lying in bed. The staff were always apologetic. I knew it wasn't their fault, but I was keen to start my second morning in a new hospital.

After they'd helped me to the bathroom, I wheeled my way down to the garden room for 'coffee club'. As I eyed up a large cake that one of the lovely volunteers had brought in, I tried not to think about the open gym session I'd missed that morning as I'd been lying in bed. At least I'd be meeting my new physio in an hour's time. With Lois's help, I slurped my dark roasted coffee through a straw and willingly accepted a few forkfuls of cake. Fed and watered, I rolled myself through the electric doors to a bright summer's day.

With Lois by my side, we wheeled around Horatio's Garden, which had been designed especially for the spinal unit. If you're imagining a few pansies and a couple of scraggy roses, think bigger, much bigger. It wouldn't have looked out of place at the Chelsea Flower Show and has even won several design awards.

The garden was planted in memory of Horatio, the son of one of the consultant orthopaedic surgeons at Salisbury. Horatio had worked as a volunteer at the spinal unit one summer and was quick to point out there should be an outside space for the patients. Tragically, at the age of 17, Horatio died while he was visiting Norway on a group trip. Shortly afterwards, his mother and father decided to build a garden at the spinal unit as part of Horatio's legacy, and some of the top names in gardening got involved. The idea spread, a charity in his name was set up and now there are four of these gardens in different spinal units around the country.

As I wheeled myself around, admiring the subtle water features and vibrant blooms, I decided that outside of rehab, this was where I would spend all of my time. The inside of the hospital had seen better days but this garden more than made up for it. I silently thanked Horatio and his family for giving me this space to relax.

All too soon, the hour was up and I rolled my way to one of the gymnasiums to meet my new physiotherapist, Kim. As Lois and I waited, we eyed up the equipment and tried to guess its use.

Through the doorway bounded a woman with long brown hair who was full of smiles for both of us.

'Hello, I'm Kim,' she said. 'I've read all your notes and I think we should get cracking.'

Half an hour later, Kim had me standing again with the help of the standing frame and we had started to plot out a course for our future physio. I instantaneously liked her and so did Lois. She had Pete's positivity and was clearly driven to get me up and walking.

At the end of the session, she took me to the computer room.

There were a few lonely desktop monitors scattered around and it was completely empty. My gaze was drawn to two other bits of equipment in the corner.

'It's a little sad, I know,' Kim said, as she read our expressions. 'Most people have an iPad or tablet now and don't come in. So that's why we decided to give it a dual use.'

She followed my gaze over to the MOTOmed and the standing frame in the corner. Newer versions than the ones in Bath and, most importantly, free of other patients.

'If I show you how to set up the MOTOmed,' Kim said, 'you could use it by yourself. I can also show Lois how to strap you into the standing frame and you can carry on with your rehab outside of our sessions.'

My eyes lit up.

I had a wheelchair. I was motivated. I had time.

These three things should have meant that I was able to work on my rehab for most of the hours outside of physio, but it didn't seem to be panning out that way.

Due to my ability to hide in a gymnasium for four hours without getting caught, I'd been fast tracked through the wheelchair process to start physio. However, I was still only allowed to stay out in it for five hours a day and I needed the wheelchair to get to the equipment. My hopes for nine to ten hours of rehab a day had slowly disappeared.

There were two barriers that I had to overcome. I had to learn how to transfer myself to the toilet and shower all by myself (Mum would be proud). I also had to start bending some rules when it came to my wheelchair time. I knew I was safe to sit in a chair for over five hours. I had enough movement to shift myself around to alleviate the pressure and I'd being doing this successfully back in Bath with no signs of pressure sores. I decided to take this decision into my own hands and spend more time in my wheelchair than was technically permitted.

By my fourth day in Salisbury Hospital I set my first lap time of the gardens at a healthy one minute, twenty-three seconds – I needed to clean up my line going into the second corner. I'd also – for the second time in my life – worked out how to transfer to, and use, the toilet and shower by myself. The first time was when I was 2 years old, and was probably done with more finesse, but luckily I wasn't being marked for style. Another chunk of my independence was wrestled back.

Fortunately, I had Kim on the case to help strengthen my hands and legs at my next session. One thing I quickly realised about this stage of my physio, was that I would be spending a large part of my time being electrocuted. Mary Shelley hadn't been far off the point when she envisaged electricity bringing about life in *Frankenstein*, because it certainly brings back life to dormant muscles.

I was lying on my front as Kim expertly applied one of the pads of the FES machine onto a nerve ending and the other on the muscle at the back of my left leg. The electrical current would then link the pads and cause a contraction.

'It won't hurt,' Kim said, as she checked the position of the pads again, 'but it will produce a tingling sensation.'

'I wouldn't tell you even if it did hurt,' I responded.

I wasn't any stranger to this little machine as I would regularly use it during my rugby career after I'd had an operation. Therefore, the thought of electrocuting myself for the afternoon didn't bring the same jitters as the tilt table had.

Kim beamed at me as she pushed the button and I felt a tingling sensation run across the back of my thigh.

'Do you think we should set a goal?' she asked. 'Something we can both aim for?'

I thought about it. Setting small goals to reach a final target is always something I've responded well to. Obviously, my ultimate aim was to make a full recovery, but I needed something smaller to work towards. A stage one and two of three steps, if you will.

'How about aiming to be discharged from hospital and being able to stand by myself, possibly walk?' I asked.

'They both sound like good things to aim for.' She pressed the button again and the tingling sensation returned.

Lying on my front, my attention was diverted by the flash of comedy monster socks that Kim had chosen for the day. They were the sort you'd receive for Christmas and possibly chuck to the back of your drawer. I wondered if she was low on laundry time at the moment.

'You'll need to do a few weekend visits first,' Kim began. 'And to be allowed home for the weekend you'll have to able to master a car transfer . . .'

I frowned guiltily as I thought of all the transfers I'd bodged over the last few days.

'Then there's a trip into town, an occupational therapist will have to visit your home and, finally, we need permission from the consultant.'

I made a mental note of these points and decided that the car transfer was the first one I'd tackle.

'Then, when you've had a few successful weekend stays, we need to think about your long-term catheter options when you're discharged. But that's much further down the line.' She pressed the button. 'We need to get you back on your feet first . . .'

I had been given the news that someone else needed my side room and I would be moved to the main ward. I'd lucked out to have it for an extra six days, so, with Mum and Lois's help, all my belongings were packed up and shifted to the eight-bed ward. I would be back with plastic curtains providing the illusion of privacy, sound muffling and solitude. The flip side of this was that, for the first time since my accident, I would be rubbing shoulders with people who had also sustained spinal injuries.

I was eager to hear everyone's story of how they'd ended up here. I'd imagined I would be meeting stunt drivers, sky diving instructors and maybe the odd matador. But, no; it turns out that people have these life-changing incidents as a matter of routine: surgery that hadn't gone as planned; a dodgy dismount from a step ladder; car and motorbike accidents. One guy had soldiered on with a bulging disc and the whole thing had exploded when he'd picked up his toddler.

I gained perspective on my life through looking at what had happened to others. And these injuries could happen to anyone. Everyone I met had been dealt a curveball and, like most curveballs, they'd happened when they were least expected and came from a direction that hadn't been anticipated. Knowing this helped me to stop blaming myself. I'd often replayed the accident, wondering what I could have done differently. Meeting other people in my position gave me permission to remove that element of blame. Accepting I had not failed in some way was a welcome release.

As I wheeled myself around my new ward and made my introductions, I scanned my new group of contemporaries. They ranged in age from late teens to late eighties. A few of them couldn't breathe by themselves so had ventilators to pump air directly into their lungs. This was life-changing in itself, as they could barely speak with this tube running into their necks.

One of the patients, Nas, had decided to show me around. He had been in Salisbury for six months and was waiting to be discharged. We stopped by two of the hospital beds where a couple of the men were lying, staring straight at their TVs. I said hello but it took a few seconds for my greeting to register with them and it was clearly a strain for them to refocus their gaze on me.

'You won't get much out of them,' Nas said, pulling his wheelchair next to mine. 'They take the maximum amount of painkillers they're allowed every morning and then wave goodbye to the day.'

'So, they just watch TV all day?' I asked.

'Yup, probably don't even try to change the channel when reruns of *Antiques Roadshow* come on.'

Motivation had left them and it seemed that no one was encouraging them to claw it back.

After thanking Nas for the tour, I rolled out of the ward. I wanted to sit in the garden, feel a bit of breeze on my skin. As I wound my way through the corridors, I started to realise how lucky I was with my current situation. Despite the doctors' initial fears, I hadn't sustained a complete spinal cord injury. There was still a chance that the messages from my brain could reach the right places.

I had also been lucky to have a strong network of family and friends that encouraged and supported my recovery. Some of the people on the ward had no one to visit them regularly, or work with them on their rehab when the physios weren't available.

It wasn't until I met other people who had similar injuries to mine that I was able to gain some perspective on my own circumstances. It's so easy to get bogged down in your own story and concerns; but when I took the time to look around, it wasn't difficult to find others who had been dealt trickier hands than my own.

The next day, my friends had messaged to make plans for the weekend. It was one of the last days of May and baking hot outside. I was fed up with being the person who'd had an accident, the person who couldn't walk, the person who had lived in a hospital for seven weeks. I didn't want to be that guy today. On the spur of the moment, I responded and told them to meet me at the closest pub. Facing a weekend of no progress, I thought that a practise roll around town would take me closer to my long-term aim of being discharged. I wanted to make this trip, whether it was supervised, authorised, sterilised or not.

When my dad and stepmum arrived, I told them my plan: we were going out, like a normal family does on a Saturday. I was expecting them to try to dissuade me but, instead, Dad nodded.

'You've been practising your car transfers with Lois,' he said. 'And it's best you try your first time out with me anyway. I can keep an eye on you.'

I had my freedom pass from a medical professional. Perhaps not from my own medical professionals, and technically Dad was an ex-medical professional, but it was close enough.

Packing up a large bag of all the things I could possibly need over the next two hours (medical gauze, anyone?), I got into my wheelchair and Dad and I made a break for it. I wish I could say that we had to hide behind laundry trolleys and nip into cleaning supplies closets to avoid detection, but that wasn't the case. We didn't see anyone on our way out and I nonchalantly glided out of the front door. Transferring to the passenger seat went as smoothly as I'd hoped and it was actually a little easier with Dad's higher car.

Driving through the countryside lanes, I had the window rolled down all the way, and was enjoying being blasted by the funnelling wind. If I could have stuck my neck-braced head out the window like Molly or Barry, I probably would've done.

'Lois told me that your physio is going well,' Dad said, as he slowed to drive over a small bridge.

'Is it weird that sometimes I'm enjoying myself?' I asked.

The highs I'd been feeling with my recent wins were helping me sail through Monday to Friday at the hospital. I'd been practising standing every day with Lois, had become proficient in using my wheelchair and was now able to shower without anyone staring at me. The wins seemed to be rolling in thick and fast at the moment.

'It's healthy,' Dad responded. 'Better than if you were resenting it.'

He was right.

As we pulled up at the pub, my excitement surged. One nifty transfer later and Dad rolled me round to the garden at the back. There, sitting in a shady corner, were three of my friends, a fresh pint in my place and a menu laid out. Bliss.

Under Kim's careful guidance I'd started to see signs of life sparking up in my left foot. One of those shy toes had started to wiggle. Although the movement was small and sporadic, it was reassuring to know that the messages were making their way down my weaker left side.

Kim had decided to up the ante by introducing me to the parallel bars. Fortunately, the ones she had in mind were a lot closer to the ground than those featured at the Olympics. The idea was that I would learn how to take my first steps while holding on to a bar with each hand.

My left leg was the main stumbling block. Despite Kim and the occupational therapist shocking it as often as they could, I had no power in my ankle, hip flexor or hamstring. This meant that I couldn't lift my foot off the ground. Think about how you walk for a moment. Now imagine trying to walk without being able to lift your foot off the ground – maybe even give it a go. Even if I could drag my leg along for any amount of time, it obviously wasn't something I could consider long-term. It would put unnecessary pressure on my right leg and I'd probably end up spending most of the day on the floor.

Maybe it might have been frustrating to know that half of my body was refusing to join in, but it didn't feel like it at this stage. I was feeling really positive about it and could see more scope for recovery. It was actually a relief to be upright and practising a walking motion – it was a huge milestone for me.

The following morning, I was informed that another essential stage in my progress would be dealt with. My catheter was going to be removed. I'd started to get some sensation back, so it was hoped that I was ready to take control of my bladder again. The curtains were pulled around my bed and the nurse gently eased the catheter out. We then had to wait for me to go 'oui oui' to check that it had worked.

It hadn't. I couldn't pee; the messages were still getting blocked. To prevent any damage to my bladder, the catheter would have to be put back in again. I was reassured that this was common, and they'd try taking it out again in a few days. I wasn't disheartened; I knew it was a first attempt. The stronger I got, the more easily the messages would flow between my brain and the rest of my body.

I listened to my playlist as the nurse put my catheter back in – a quick-fix distraction while something uncomfortable was happening. At the end of my playlist, I looked up. The nurse was frowning.

'I'm just going to get a colleague,' she said, before disappearing behind the curtain around my bed.

Five minutes later, an older nurse came back, and I started my playlist up again. Halfway through, I realised something wasn't right. There was a poking and tugging sensation that was bordering on painful.

'I'm just going to find the matron,' the senior nurse said. 'She'll know what to do.'

Fifteen minutes later, the matron of the ward was by my side. She took a quick look and then had a go herself.

'It's getting stuck towards the end,' the matron said. 'I think there's a false passage. Don't worry, it's very common. But I'm just going to get a doctor.'

Half an hour later, the curtain was snapped back by one of the registrars for the spinal unit. Plastic gloves were put on and she got to work. I tried to watch a film on my iPad in an attempt to block out the three people around my bed who were all intently focused on one very specific part of me. For once I was actually grateful for having no sensation down there.

'I'm just going to get the consultant,' the registrar said, after admitting defeat. 'She's on her rounds, but I'll grab her as soon as I can.'

An hour passed.

'Right, let's see what I can do,' the consultant said, as she leant closer. I was on my second film now and fifth catheter fitting.

The consultant was a little more forceful, maybe because she was more confident in her abilities as head of the ward. Twenty minutes later I glanced down. It didn't seem to be going well. I was sweating from the continuous procedures and just wanted a shower and a bit of peace. And to pee.

'I'm just going to contact a colleague in the urology ward,' the consultant said, while removing her gloves.

Ninety minutes later, in rode a consultant urologist to hopefully save the day.

I braced myself for more prodding and poking as I eyed up the small instrument with a bend at the end that he had brought with him. Hmmm . . .

I took my mind away, thought of the Pacific Coast, Lois, the adventures we'd had and might have again. Anything to not be here.

'All done,' the consultant urologist said. 'I managed to get the tube past the false passage created by the last catheter and it's in place now.'

Five and a half hours had passed, and I was back to where I was first thing that morning.

Sometimes, though, you have to take the rough with the smooth. Not every step takes you forwards; sometimes you have to turn around and start again.

CHAPTER 10

THE SMALL STUFF

'And you're sure you are ready for this?' Mum asked, as she helped wrestle me into my swimming shorts. 'It isn't too soon, is it? It might be too soon . . .'

'I'm looking forward to it,' I responded, as I tried to help her by lifting my left leg with my arms.

It was time to get back in the water. Kim was keen to start hydrotherapy with me, which is a fancy way of saying 'exercising in a swimming pool'. The irony of using a pool to help me recover from an accident I'd had in a pool was not lost on me. I probably should have been apprehensive, maybe even scared, about getting back into water, but I didn't feel that way. I've always loved water and nearly concentrated on swimming rather than rugby in my early teenage years. People should face their fears, not bury them. Also, I'd like to clarify that I'm not poolist. The swimming pool in Salisbury had never wronged me and odds were that it would stay that way. I've dived into thousands of pools and only one has had it in for me.

Swimming shorts on, I chucked a T-shirt over the top and wheeled myself down to the pool to meet Kim. She was standing next to what looked like another torture device. It was a mechanised chair that was bolted to the edge of the pool with straps across it. I can only assume that it was originally designed for quadriplegics who were suspected of being witches.

Sitting in my new chair, I was slowly lowered into the water. It felt good. I was beginning to recognise different sensations across parts of my skin and the soft touch of the water was familiar and welcome. Kim hopped into the pool and positioned an inflatable ring with a rope attached to it under me. Our first task was to help me acclimatise to the water and see if I could start kicking. Leading the way, Kim walked in a circle around the pool, pulling the rope as I serenely sailed after her. I felt a bit like a show pooch at Crufts. I gave a few little kicks and noticed how much stronger my right leg was compared to my left one.

Next, I was manoeuvred so that I was upright. The warm water supported my limbs and I experienced an ease of movement that I hadn't felt in a long while. In the shallow end, we practised kneeling and strengthening my core. Kim then suggested we try something that I'd been waiting for.

Holding on to both of my hands, she guided me forwards. Right leg leading, followed by the left, I took my first tentative steps. I closed my eyes for a moment and imagined that I was nimbly weaving my way down a busy high street. No one stared at me – I was just a man getting from A to B.

Later that afternoon, I wheeled myself into the computer room to have a go on the standing frame by myself. Another patient, Rick, who was in his late thirties and was also in a wheelchair was using the MOTOmed. He'd frequently be in the gym at the same time as me and we'd struck up a friendship, motivating each other to keep going with our rehab.

'Afternoon,' Rick said, popping his head around from the

MOTOmed. 'I saw you did another lap of the gardens yesterday. Set a good time?'

'One minute, two seconds. I want to get under the minute mark tomorrow if I can,' I responded, lining up my wheelchair in front of the standing frame.

Rick let out a low whistle. 'I think that must be the best time for the quadriplegics.'

My garden laps had caught on. We'd all decided on an official circuit that took us around the central island of flowers with the trellis archway being the start and finishing point. I'd often sit out in the sunshine watching the other patients try to beat their best times. Even a couple of guys in the electric wheelchairs had joined in. I admired their nerves of steel as they gamely took the corners in their bulky, motorised wheelchairs.

'I'm still hovering just below the minute mark,' Rick added. 'It should be lower than that. It's that big bush on the last corner. I always lose my nerve and swerve too far to the left to avoid it.'

Rick was paraplegic so had retained the strength in his upper body, unlike me. He'd injured his lower back picking up one of his children and was desperate to get home to his family. He worked hard every day and set high standards for himself.

I pulled myself up and tried to hold myself steady. 'Ah, yes, the "Rhododendron of Doom". It's taken many a good man out.'

Standing was getting easier, compared to my first wobbly attempt back in Bath. I tried to hold myself still and took a deep breath. As long as I could avoid a spasm in my left leg and had something solid to hold on to, I was now able to stand unassisted. This also meant that I had finally recovered the advantage of being able to pee standing up once my catheter was removed. As well as going to the toilet, having the strength in my core to stand helped me with transfers, reaching things, seeing over hedges and scaring people who hadn't seen me for a while – all important skills.

Exactly two months after my accident, the hospital gave me a present by taking off the white plate that covered the top of my chest. It had been my constant, weighty companion since my accident. It made my skin itch when it was hot outside and sleeping uncomfortable. I still had to wear my neck brace, but I felt so much lighter and freer without half a stormtrooper outfit on. Although I was much more vulnerable to lightsaber attacks, it was a risk that I was willing to take for the comparative comfort it provided.

I had a new enemy now anyway – The Sneeze. When I'd first arrived at Salisbury, the other patients would greet me in an untraditional manner, 'Morning, did you sleep well? Have you sneezed yet?' Their question made complete sense to me as a spinal injury patient. Sneezes were no longer an annoyance, they were fearful. A ball of energy blasting up your spine is not something you want to dabble in. I had therefore come up with several elaborate ways of either preventing sneezes or holding them in. If neither of these worked, I would screw my face up and sneeze like a dog to reduce any damage.

The first night spent without my body armour on, I was caught up in a surprise sneezing fit. On they went as I screwed up my face and tried to minimise the damage. The next morning, I could feel that something wasn't right. Explaining what had happened to a nurse, I was told that I couldn't have physio that morning, had to stay in bed for most of the day and might need a scan. All because of a sneeze.

That evening I was given the all-clear to leave my bed, so I wheeled myself down to the communal TV room. Ten wheelchairs were positioned in a line in front of the TV. I backed myself into a space between Rick and Nas. *Top Gear* was on and I settled back to admire the cars I couldn't afford and which were so low I probably wouldn't be able to get out of. If someone gifted me one, I'd just have to live in it.

I looked up to see Souto coming through the door. He'd regularly drive down in the evenings after work to sit with me either in the garden or TV room. I lifted my arm to greet him.

'All right, Ed?' he said, as he entered with a large bag of Doritos tucked under his arm.

He stood in front of us and went down the line, fist bumping each of us in turn. 'All right, Nas, Rick, Claire, Laura, Dom . . .'

Souto stopped in front of Dom, his hand stretched out as Dom stared at it.

'Sorry, mate,' Souto said, 'forgot you can't move your arm.'

I winced as Souto went to fist bump Dom's forehead instead. Dom didn't seem to mind and made an effort to move his head to meet Souto halfway. Souto carried on down the line greeting each of them in turn and remembering everyone's name before taking a seat in the middle.

'What are we watching, lads?' he asked, as he opened his bag of crisps.

'*Top Gear*,' Dom responded. 'They're taking a road trip across Cuba.'

I only half listened as Souto and Dom discussed which cars they wanted. I'd been distracted by something out of the corner of my eye. Nas was tapping his foot along to the music playing over the top of the programme.

'Nas,' I said, 'your foot's moving.'

'Oh, yeah? I can move it a bit.'

'But you told me you'd never walk again. If you can move your foot then there might still be a chance.'

Rick peered over at Nas's foot. 'It's definitely tapping.'

'Why don't you come down to the gym with me and Rick tomorrow morning?'

'Nah, no point,' Nas said. 'Just waiting for my flat to be fixed so I can get my wheelchair in.'

Nas had been left paraplegic after a car accident and had been told early on that it was very unlikely he would walk again. Since then he'd given up hope of any sort of recovery. He wasn't on great terms with a lot of the staff, but was always friendly to the patients. He refused to take part in physio as he didn't see the point if he wouldn't be able to walk again. He'd been waiting to be discharged for the last two months while his flat was being made wheelchair accessible.

'Come on, mate,' Rick said. 'There's not much else to do around here.'

'Pick you up at nine?' I said to Nas.

He sighed. 'Okay, but I'm only doing an hour.'

'Fine by me,' I responded, pleased that we'd at least get him down to the gym.

The next afternoon I made my way over to physio with Kim. As promised, Nas had been ready by nine that morning and had followed Rick and me down to the gym. I'd shown him what exercises might help, Rick put on some terrible Eighties music and all three of us began our circuits of reps. Chatting over the top of the music, I suggested that I'd ask my mum to make us some sweatbands and then we could do a proper Eighties montage. Nas seemed to enjoy himself and even said he would come back with us the next day.

I smiled to myself as Lois and I entered the larger rehab room. Eyeing up Kim's sock choice of the day (Bart Simpson), I wheeled myself over to the parallel bars.

'I've thought of a way I could get a few more sessions of hydrotherapy. Once a week really isn't enough,' I said, as Kim checked my posture. 'What if I joined the onsite gym as a member of the public? I could then have access to the pool during the public swimming times. If Lois was with me, it would be safe.'

Kim and I were always coming up with ways to get around the system so I could have more rehab time. I was definitely thinking outside the box with this one. The pool at the spinal unit was also used as public leisure facilities. People from the spinal unit had limited access to the pool so as not to disturb the gym members and baby classes. But there was nothing to stop me joining the gym and having access to the pool.

'Technically there would be nothing stopping you,' Kim said, as she repositioned my leg.

'I'll roll down there and sign up today,' I responded, as I held onto the parallel bars with both hands. 'How long until you think I'll be able to visit home for a weekend?'

'It's not up to me, but not long now. Maybe even next week if we can get the consultant to agree to it.'

Staring down at my legs, I willed them to do what I was asking of them. I was getting stronger, but the same issues were persisting. My left leg still had a lot of spasticity and there was no power in my ankle and very little in my hamstring or hip flexor. Either Lois or Kim had to lift my left leg for me to be able to take a step forwards and we hadn't got any further than this in the past week. I was starting to get frustrated at my lack of progress.

'Let's try the high lunge again,' Kim said, helping me change position.

Putting my left leg forwards, I held the position. Until a spasm hit.

My left leg wobbled and then crumpled beneath me. I could feel myself toppling to the side. Everything went into slow motion. With nothing to break my fall, I tried to grab for something to hold me upright, but my movements were too slow, my arms too weak. I felt my knee jar as I hit the floor.

Not again. Please, not again.

I lay on the floor for a moment as Kim checked me over and Lois held my hand. As I'd fallen, Kim had leapt to protect my neck and head. Another knock in the wrong place might have been catastrophic. Kim was asking the questions I was so used to now: 'Can you feel this? Can you squeeze that?' My knee felt sore, but I knew it could have been so much worse.

'That was a close one,' Kim said, once she was satisfied that I could be helped back into my wheelchair.

'Bloody spasms,' I responded, as I used my arms to lift my legs onto the wheelchair's footplates.

The spasms could come at any time and rendered my leg useless. That was fine if I was in bed or sitting up in my wheelchair, but if I was standing, my leg could just give way beneath me. Even if I did manage to take a few steps by myself, I couldn't risk walking outside of physio as a spasm could send me flying forwards at any time.

The next morning, I had to admit to myself that there was

something seriously wrong with my knee. It was twice the size of my right one and was throbbing. After a very painful transfer to the toilet I knew that I would have to tell the ward doctor about it. During the night, I'd been hoping it was just a sprain that would heal up in a couple of days, but I knew now that it was much more serious than that.

As Lois went to find one of the ward doctors, I thought about my situation and what a delay to my recovery could do. The very thought of staying in this hospital for months on end made my heart sink. I wanted to be in my own space, able to work to my own schedule. What I wanted was to go home.

Lois interrupted my thoughts when she returned with the ward doctor, Anna. Every so often in life you meet someone who is bloody brilliant at their job. I'd been lucky enough to have met two of these already, Pete and Kim. Anna also had this special quality. Within a couple of hours of looking at my knee, she had spoken to the radiographers about it, organised an X-ray and persuaded the radiographers to consider an MRI scan if my knee didn't improve.

Diligent doctors aside, I was still laid up in bed with strict instructions that I couldn't do any physio or rehab for at least a week. My recovery had been put on hold.

Lying in bed that night, I began to fret about my situation. Always at the back of my mind was the worry that I was missing my window of recovery. A few weeks laid up might mean that I wouldn't be able to walk by myself. A bad knock to my weaker knee might mean a wheelchair for life. The stakes were that high. I went through my routine of trying to calm myself by watching a film and posting about my day, but nothing was working. These thoughts and worries wouldn't leave me. My breathing was getting quicker and shallower, my head was whirling. The stress I was feeling was beginning to ratchet upwards into panic. On and on it went.

Squeezing my eyes shut, I tried to gain some perspective. I looked at myself only five days after the accident. I wanted to reach out to that Ed – to hear how he would be handling this . . .

'I've had a really shit day,' I told Ed then, as I thought of him in the hospital bed. 'I think this is as far as our recovery will go.'

'So, we're going to be stuck like this?' he responded. 'Just a bit of movement in the right arm . . . That's not what I was expecting. I'd hoped we'd get back more . . .'

'Oh, no, no,' I said hurriedly. 'I didn't mean to worry you like that. We're much further ahead. I'm in a wheelchair. Set a blistering 45-second lap time round the gardens yesterday. I can stand by myself. But I've got stuck taking steps, I can't do it. I can't lift my foot by myself. And today I had a fall in physio and hurt my knee. It's pretty bad, even bigger than after that dodgy scrum when we were—'

'Wait! So, I'll be able to stand again?'

'Yes, but we might not be able to walk. There's still a chance, but it feels like it's slipping away . . .'

He sighed. 'Do you not remember the promise we made in the first week in hospital?'

'Yes . . .'

'That night when we promised that we'd accept being in a wheelchair for the rest of our life, if we could just have the use of our arms and hands back. We'd be independent then, not a burden to Lois or Mum—'

'Yes,' I interjected, as he didn't know the full situation, 'but being in a wheelchair is still bloody hard: there are the kerbs; everything is designed so badly for wheelchair users; my arms are still so weak; and I'm constantly staring at everyone's crotch . . .'

'You expect sympathy from me? I'm just lying here. I'm basically a head on a pillow.'

'Yes, but—'

'No buts. It's less than three months since the accident and you can stand. You've got further than we ever imagined you would. Yes, you've twisted your knee and you might be laid up for a bit, but that doesn't mean our recovery is over. And even if it is, accept what you have now. It's more than we thought we had the right to bargain for.'

'I know,' I said, suitably chastised. 'I just miss home.'

'Me too.'

I blinked my eyes open. Head on a pillow . . . Ed was right; I had come so far in only nine weeks. I opened up my phone and looked at all the videos that had been taken of me over the last couple of months. Quietly watching them, I was glad that I had gained some internal perspective. By looking back over my own progress, I was able to see how far I had come.

It was time to refocus on the small stuff and appreciate how lucky I was to be able to whinge about my walking technique at all.

Over the next few days, I went and picked Nas up in the mornings and took him to meet Rick in the gym. My knee throbbed, but I could still work on my upper body strength. Afterwards, we went back to my new ward and surveyed what food Mum had brought in for us. She still visited most days, and still brought half of the M&S food hall with her.

As I finished my mid-morning sandwich, I reached over and picked up a plastic fork that came with one of the salad bowls. Jamming it down the inside of my neck brace, I gave it a wiggle. The relief was instantaneous. My neck was so itchy from the summer heat that I would regularly be found with a pen or chopstick stuck down there.

Remembering to remove the plastic fork, I headed off to meet the wheelchair dealer for my late-morning appointment. The fact that this appointment had been organised for me was a sobering thought – I would obviously need to be in a wheelchair for a considerable amount of time. Fortunately, the Matt Hampson Foundation had offered to pay for one for me. I was very grateful to them as the alternatives were either borrowing a clunky NHS one or paying for my own and that could cost thousands of pounds.

I sat patiently as Noel took all my measurements and made a note of them.

'So, have you had a chance to look through the catalogue and make your pick?' he asked, looking up from his notebook.

'I've been doing some research and, well, the choices are endless . . . I know I want a lightweight, active one that I can transfer in and out of easily.'

'Well, that narrows it down a bit,' he said, pulling open a few pages of the catalogue.

There was also another part of me that I had to acknowledge. I was 28 years old and I wanted one that was a bit cool. I didn't want to look like I was rolling around in my granddad chair back in Bath hospital. The wheelchair I had at the moment was gigantic and had the turning circle of the

Titanic. I wanted to be nimble. It would also be nice to be mistaken for a participant in the Paralympics. Was that too much to ask?

Together we pored over the options, but I couldn't seem to narrow it down. It seemed like such a monumental decision. What if I made the wrong one? In the end, I decided to hold off until I had a chance to message a few other people with spinal cord injuries who I'd met on Instagram to get their advice.

It was Friday and a weekend of no physio or rehab lay in front of me. I decided to take some action. I wheeled around the corridors until I found the nice ward doctor, Anna, who I knew would be sympathetic to my request. I set out my case and she agreed that it was a good one. She would support the request to stay at my dad's house for the weekend, but there were still a couple of things I would have to do. We divided them up between us and Anna set off to find the consultant to ask her to consider granting permission. I wheeled myself back to my ward, and Lois and I set off for my first 'official' trip into town and to show the nurses my car transfer. Dad and my stepmum, Sue, went to find the occupational therapist so they could arrange a time for her to visit their home.

Everyone had swung into action. It was going to be tight and we only had one afternoon to get everything done, but at least we were trying. I really needed this. I needed to go home.

My excitement bubbled as Dad unlocked the front door and pushed it open for me. He stood aside to let me be the first to enter.

'In you go then, Ed. I've set up a bed in my study for you. I think there's everything you'll need in there.'

Wheeling myself though the wide door, I remembered

how lucky I was that my dad and Sue had built their own home a couple of years ago and no longer lived in a house that was over two hundred years old. Like most modern buildings, the doors of their home were wide and all the floor joints were flush. Getting around in a wheelchair was a relative breeze in a home like this one.

Lois followed me inside and ushered me into the study.

All of them had done their best to make it as welcoming as possible. Dad's study and a toilet were on the ground floor of the house. The kitchen, living room and all the bedrooms were on the floors above. Through the door of the study, I stared at the flight of stairs that led to the rest of the house.

'We can hang out in the garden,' Sue said. 'Your dad will cook you whatever you want. And it's warm enough to eat outside. If it gets chilly, we can all sit down here in the study. There's enough room.'

'It looks great,' I said. 'I really appreciate all the effort you've gone too.'

Five minutes later, I wheeled myself out of the study to investigate the bathroom situation. With my back to the others, I looked mournfully up at the stairs that led to every other room in the house. I felt a bit like my dog, Barry, when he was a puppy and I was trying to train him to sleep downstairs. That hadn't lasted long; he'd soon found a way to get up them . . .

'Daaad . . .'

'Yes, Ed?'

'If we could get me safely to the floor . . . I could then slowly bum shuffle up the stairs . . . If you and Lois could then lift my wheelchair up the stairs, I could stay up there for most of the weekend . . .'

Whilst my dad and Lois exchanged glances, I gave them my best, Barry-inspired puppy eyes.

'You're going to do it anyway, aren't you, Ed?' Dad said, as he offered me his arm. 'Lois, you take the other side.'

Fifteen minutes later, having used my arms to lift myself up each step, I had made it to the top. Looking around at the familiar sights of Dad and Sue's house, the open-plan living room and kitchen, the bowls of flowers where Dad always placed them, I took in a deep breath and smiled.

It might not have been my house but, with Lois and my family there with me, it felt like home.

CHAPTER 11

HOMEWARD BOUND

'You'll be able to come back soon,' Dad said, as I stared out of the car window while he drove me back to the hospital.

'I know,' I responded, trying to focus on his words, 'but what I really want is to be discharged.'

With my first night away from hospital ticked off, I was now completely focused on being discharged. The average hospital stay for a patient with my injuries is four to six months, sometimes longer. I was aiming to be discharged in under three. I was incredibly lucky that Restart, the charity that supported rugby players, was still keen to pay for my physiotherapy. Having spoken to Pete and Kim, they had both agreed to work with me on a private basis and had capacity to see me several times a week. Ironically, I would actually have more access to rehab once I left hospital than I was currently having.

'Sue and I have been talking about that,' Dad responded. 'You and Lois would be more than welcome to come and stay with us. The house in Cardiff isn't very suitable for a wheelchair. Much better that you're with us.'

I took a moment to think about it; it made complete sense. Their house could have been designed for a wheelchair user with its wide hallways and flush flooring. Even better, it had its own gym as Sue was a personal trainer. I would be able to work on my rehab eight hours a day if I wanted to.

'Thanks, Dad,' I responded, a plan already beginning to form. 'I'll have to ask Lois but I'm sure she'll agree. This could be perfect.'

Something else was also becoming a possibility: I might actually be able to make it to New York to see Fleetwood Mac in six weeks' time. I was still in a wheelchair with a catheter, but that didn't prevent me from flying if the consultant would agree to it. What better way to persuade her to grant permission than showing I was able to function outside of hospital for a month? Now all I had to do was actually get myself discharged. I'd ticked off everything on the list and was just waiting for my catheter to be removed.

A few days later, the swelling on my knee had gone down so I was able to go back to physio with Kim. Whilst I'd been away, she had arranged for me to have a fitting for a FES contraption that would help lift my left foot. With the wires in the correct place on my left leg, the FES would monitor my movements through a pressure sensor under my heel. When it was time for my left leg to lift up it would send a pulse of electricity through my leg, causing the muscles to contract and my foot to raise. This meant that Lois was now out of a job as my Chief Foot Raiser. I didn't think she minded too much as she was busy preparing for her well-deserved netball trip to New Zealand.

As Kim strapped the FES to my leg, I held onto the parallel bars for support.

'There we go,' she said, while straightening. 'You're all set. Want to give it a test run?'

I gave her a grin in response.

One hand on each side of the bars, I stepped forwards with my right leg. There was a second's pause and then my left foot also lifted fractionally off the ground, just enough for me to move my leg forwards. The timing of the electrical currents wasn't perfect and didn't raise my foot very far, so my step was out of time and my gait wasn't very smooth. It didn't matter. Right foot first and then my slightly lagging left foot following – I was walking!

That Sunday, Lois and I had decided to visit a pub together for a late lunch. It was one of those pubs with rolling lawns out the back that are designed to make you want to stay for fifteen minutes longer, take in the view, and chat about anything and everything.

'It's getting harder to go back, isn't it?' Lois said.

I had been nursing the last of my pint for twenty minutes, not wanting the afternoon to end.

'Is it that obvious?' I asked, lifting the glass to my mouth.

She smiled at me. 'Only to someone who knows that it doesn't take you an hour and a half to drink a pint.'

'One more for the road?' I asked, waggling my glass at her.

'Two whole pints on a Sunday?' she said smiling. 'They'll have you done for drink driving your wheelchair.'

I raised my eyebrows at her in protest but she was already standing up to go to the bar.

An hour later than we had expected, we reluctantly agreed to head back to the car park. Rather than having to take my wheelchair through the busy pub, Lois wheeled me around to the side of the garden as we chatted about when the doctors would finally remove my catheter. The lawn's incline was getting steeper and Lois stopped for a moment to eye it up.

'Perhaps we should go back,' Lois said, as she looked around her and smiled at the group of men sitting the other side of a large oak tree.

I assessed the situation. We were halfway up a hillock, more of a mound really, but for a wheelchair user even the smallest gradient change on an uneven surface was something to think about. The world is designed for people who walk rather than roll. In the old days, Lois and I wouldn't have even commented on this, let alone stopped and stared at it. I'd thought that stairs would be my only trouble in a wheelchair, but I was wrong. When we visited the town centre I would have to wheel down a pavement, completely in the wrong direction so I could find a dropped kerb, as I lacked the upper body strength to 'hop' my wheelchair up a kerb. Often there wasn't a dropped kerb on the other side of the road, so I'd have to wheel along the edge, cars veering out of my way, until I found another dropped kerb and could join the safety of the pavement again. Then I'd wheel back down the pavement to the point that I wanted to arrive at. It was a faffy, zigzag way of getting around and it was very annoying.

The incline in front of us wasn't that steep; we'd done similar before and it would take ten minutes to get me up to the back doors of the pub again. I'd then have to get through the busy pub, trying not to hit people's ankles with my metal chair.

'Just go for it,' I said to Lois, after saying hello to a couple who were walking down the mound. 'Step on it.'

Lois pushed me up the mound at a reasonable pace. It was going really well, until the footplate of my wheelchair dug into the grass and jolted to a sudden stop.

Flying forwards, I only had time to move my arms in front of me to protect my neck.

I landed with a thump on my front and the air whooshed out of me.

There was a pause, where even the birds in the trees seemed to hush for a moment to stare down at me. And then chaos erupted.

The four men who were sitting the other side of the tree from us scrabbled to their feet and ran towards us. Over the top of their shouted questions was the trace of a scream from a woman in the pub garden. Chairs scraped back on the patio and people rushed towards us.

Blocking out these sounds, I made a quick check of myself, wiggling everything that needed to wiggle and gently testing my neck. I was fine. I made a grab for the tree and tried to pull myself up. Straining to heave myself upright, I had to give in. I wasn't strong enough and slid down onto my front again.

Lois was down by my side in a flash. 'Are you okay, Ed?'

'Yes, I'm fine,' I mumbled into the grass.

'I'm so sorry,' she continued. 'I didn't know the footplates could get stuck like that.'

I summoned all of my strength and tried again to pull myself up with my right hand. It was no good. I slid back down again, exhausted. I didn't have the strength.

The sound of footsteps sliding to a stop near to my head made me flinch.

'Oh my God,' one of the men said to Lois. 'We saw it happen from over there.'

Another man knelt down next to me. 'Can you hear me?' Before he waited for an answer, he lifted his head and shouted, 'Someone call for an ambulance.'

'No!' I said, as loudly as I could. 'I'm fine. Please don't call for an ambulance. It's not necessary.'

'Should we roll him?' one of the men said to another. 'Perhaps someone here is a doctor and could help.'

'Oh, that poor, poor man,' a woman said from further away.

My cheeks burned with shame as a small crowd gathered around me, all discussing what they should do. I was still lying flat on my face and all they could see of me was the back of my neck-braced head and my backside.

'I just need help getting back into my wheelchair,' I said.

Only Lois seemed to hear me.

'We just need to get him back into his wheelchair,' she said, as calmly as she could.

Everyone stopped talking and turned to her. She pointed at the two biggest men. 'You two. If you could hold Ed under each arm, I'll support his head.

She bent down next to me and put a hand on either side of my neck. 'It's okay,' she whispered. 'It'll be over in a moment.'

I felt myself being lifted and then straightened. Someone pushed the wheelchair towards me and I was able to take a step back and sit down in it.

I looked up to meet all of their gazes. Some grass was still stuck to my face and Lois stepped forwards to brush it away. Everyone stared back at me – some were wide-eyed with shock, others were frowning in concern.

'Is there someone I can call?' a man asked, holding out his phone. 'A friend or relative?'

'No, no. It's fine. Thank you,' I said.

When they wouldn't part to let me through, I realised they needed more before they'd let this wheelchair-bound man depart. 'Thanks for your help. Very much appreciated. Will be on my way now. Thanks again.'

My cheeks were still burning from the embarrassment of it all, but I had to force that down to smile at them reassuringly.

Lois moved behind me and pushed the wheelchair over the peak of the mound. I could feel fifteen sets of eyes on the back of my head as the misbehaving wheelchair juddered into the car park.

We were both quiet on the drive back to hospital. That feeling of helplessness had stayed with me and I couldn't shake it off. I was 28 and had become either the object of pity or panic. There was no middle ground for me. I stared out of the window and for the first time in weeks, tears began to form. I quickly blinked them away before Lois saw them.

It was the first time I had encountered the general public's reaction to something happening to a disabled person. Back in the cocoon of hospital, I was normal, one of many patients amongst his peers. We all misjudged our transfers sometimes and took a tumble. The medical staff were used to it, so they reacted calmly, checked us over and put it aside. Outside of that environment, my fall had become a tragedy, something people would tell their friends and family about. I knew they had all meant well. I knew they were good people, but their reaction had reduced me to feeling like a victim or a child. Someone who wasn't spoken to, only about. Never before had I experienced people panicking about me – I was supposed to be the kindly, young man who helped others out.

Still staring out of the window, I reached over and took Lois's hand. I gave it a squeeze. 'I want to walk again.'

She gave it a squeeze back. 'I know.'

I had ticked off everything on the list. All that stood between me and being discharged was having my catheter removed.

After the last attempt to remove it, I'd been told that they would try again in a few days. Three weeks had passed, and I'd been informed that because of the complications last time, they wanted to perform a cystoscopy so they could check on the false passage that had been created. That was fine – better safe than sorry – but, since then, I'd had no word on when this would happen. My sensation was improving down there and I wanted to have another crack at having my catheter removed. I'd waited three weeks, frustration starting to nibble at me. In the end, I persuaded my consultant to chase up urology.

Finally, there was some news: it would be at least another three weeks until I could have the urodynamics test, a small, routine procedure that I needed.

I mulled over what to do before pulling out my iPad and typing out a message on Instagram:

I don't know what is going on and why no one can/ will perform this simple procedure for me, all I know is that I feel caught up in something bigger and I'm helpless to do anything about it. I feel sorry for the nurses, doctors and other staff who struggle with the inefficiencies of the system, but most of all I feel sorry for the people actually suffering at the hands of it. Somebody somewhere is waiting for my bed to start their rehab and they are having to delay their recovery as a knock-on effect of my situation. That doesn't sit well with me.

The next morning, I was told that there had been a cancellation in urology and they could perform the cystoscopy that afternoon.

I was always aware that the odds were stacked in my favour.

My dad used to work as a GP so understood how the NHS worked, my blog had gained some attention and I had a supportive circle of friends and family. On this occasion I had used my blog to show the hospital that they had fallen down on this point. I knew they were reading it, as early on in my stay the head of marketing had come and introduced herself. Nothing was said, but she made it clear that the hospital was aware of the blog and hoped that my stay was going well.

My problem with urology was quickly ironed out when I pushed for it through a medium the hospital was wary of – my blog. If I hadn't done this, I could have been in hospital for another three to six weeks.

As well as sometimes lacking joined-up thinking between the departments, the NHS is woefully underfunded. We are all aware of that. We are also understandably proud of our NHS and accept the mantra that it gives us the best possible care. The provision of free national healthcare is something to value. But when the system is broken, then it cannot provide the best possible care. Knowing this, I was left in a bizarre position with a couple of the doctors when I was asking for more physio.

Often, with my dad by my side, I would ask them outright, 'Would more physio help my recovery?' Most of them would admit that it would, but a couple tried to tell me that it wouldn't, that there was no evidence that more than three hours of physio a week would help. This is not true. The vast majority of studies show that early intervention and volume is what people with spinal injuries need to make the maximum recovery. They had tried to use their status as 'doctor' to override what I knew to be true and many of their colleagues had admitted to me was correct.

As I spent more time in an open ward, it became apparent

that others didn't have my benefits and privileges. Patients would accept what they were told, that extra physio wouldn't help them, that the aim was to get them into a wheelchair and no mention was made of them walking. It wasn't that the individuals who worked in the NHS were happy with this arrangement; it was the system that constrained them so they couldn't provide the full spectrum of rehab that the patients needed. Understandably, some of the medical staff would become frustrated with these constraints and move to the private sector. The NHS was leaking valuable members of its profession.

It all comes down to funding. There is no 'National' in the NHS. Each region is split into separate hospital trusts and each is competing for limited funding with growing demand. Therefore, to access funding, the hospitals have to satisfy certain criteria. Like schools who are forced to show their worth through exam results, I have been told that spinal units gain their funding through turnover. This suggests that a hospital may be under pressure to get a patient into a wheelchair and out the door as quickly as possible. I had often wondered where I would be if I had accepted my original prognosis.

Whilst the NHS is waiting for more funding, an avenue to consider is what other resources the patients have, such as friends and family who are able to help them with their physio. However, it must be remembered that many people don't have friends or family who are able to visit regularly because of work or family commitments. As with most things in life, not all avenues are open to everyone.

In two days everything had flipped. I had gone from facing another three to six weeks in hospital to being discharged the next day. Mum and Dad rallied the troops, and everyone shifted up a gear to get me ready to leave hospital. Lois had already reluctantly left for the airport for her netball tour in New Zealand. She had hesitated when she realised that I would be discharged just as she was leaving, but I urged her to go. We'd have plenty of time to spend together outside of hospital once she returned.

After eighty days in hospital, I was a free man. My last night was spent in the TV room with the other patients, enjoying the camaraderie that came naturally to a group of people all in the same boat. Excitement coiled inside of me and I barely slept that night, even with the ear plugs and T-shirt draped over my head that I had come to rely on to block out the sounds and sights of the ward.

At 8 a.m., Dad, Sue and my brother Josh came to shift all my stuff into their convoy of cars while I wheeled around thanking the staff and saying my goodbyes to the other patients. It was one of those moments that I made a conscious effort to remember: my last day as a patient.

When I arrived at Dad and Sue's house, my old bedroom upstairs had already been set up for me and I bum shuffled my way up the steps. Arriving at the top, I gave a wide grin when I clocked the huge spread Dad and Sue had prepared for my arrival. Mountains of sandwiches had been balanced on serving dishes surrounded by smaller plates of pork pies, sausage rolls and deli meats. At the head of the table sat the customary giant chocolate cake that Sue insisted on for any form of family celebration or gathering, even breakfasts. As I made a beeline for a pork pie, I hoped they realised they'd set a standard now and 'Buffet Wednesday' would become a weekly fixture.

Friends arrived to join the celebration and I was immediately relieved of my wheelchair so they could attempt to pull some wheelies. There was even a present for me that I hadn't been expecting. Some of my dad's friends had set up a crowd-funding page to help with accommodation and flights for the trip to New York. It looked like it was becoming a possibility. I had something to aim for, something to look forward to. The day was everything that I'd hoped it would be.

The next morning, I was suddenly alone. Life had returned to normal for everyone else; they had to go to work or attend to the many errands that had been neglected after months of postponing everything to visit me in hospital. Wheeling myself onto the patio, I parked my wheelchair next to the outdoor dining table and gazed out over the view of the Mendips. I'm naturally a sociable person but being by myself was bliss. There would be days in hospital where I wouldn't have any visitors and the ward would seem quiet, but I was never really on my own. There was always a doctor, nurse, health assistant, volunteer or patient only a few feet way. I suppose I never really valued personal space until I didn't have any.

Staring out over the rolling hills, my thoughts naturally turned to my future. I wasn't so blinded by the progress of my recovery to think that I would ever return to playing professional rugby. That realisation had come quite early on to me. People had expected me to be distraught by this revelation, and that I would heavily mourn the career I had worked so hard for. That wasn't the case. I was 28 years old and had played professional rugby for ten years. Like all professional sports people, rugby players have a short shelf-life. You would do well

Playing for Wasps in 2014.

Tony Marshall/Stringer/Gettyimages sport Gettyimages

Narrowly escaping a
tackle from Bundee Aki
when playing for the
Dragons in 2016.

Huw Evans Picture Agency

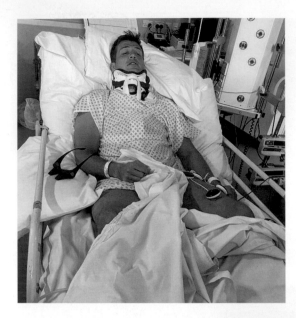

Left: 9 April 2017, my second day in intensive care.

Below: 18 April 2017, my tenth day in intensive care and the first time that I was able to go outside. I was so happy to see my dogs, Barry and Molly.

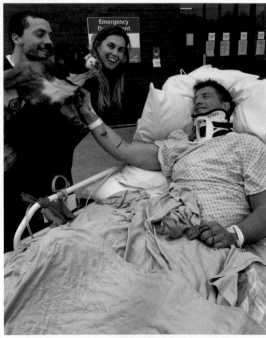

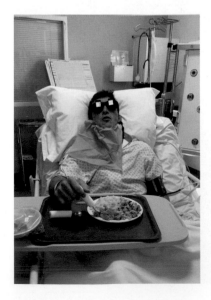

The legendary Lay-Z-Readers. These glasses used mirrors to allow me to see around the room, so that I could look at more than just up people's noses.

Eating dinner on the tilt table in Helena Ward while Molly looks on in May 2017.

Using a zimmer frame as a makeshift bench press with the support of Pete, Lois and friends at the Royal United Hospital in Bath.

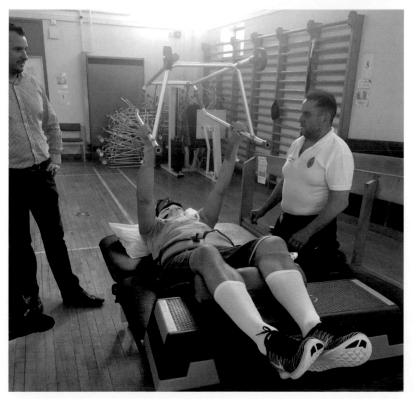

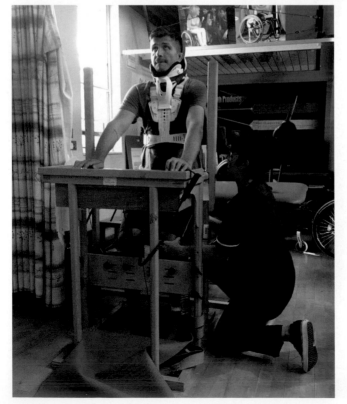

Top left: Using a MOTOmed in Salisbury's specialist spinal unit.

Top right: 28 May 2017, my first trip to the pub since my accident, with Dad and Souto.

Left: Practising standing again with the help of Kim in Salisbury.

My first 'off piste' adventure with Pete and Wyn, August 2017.

Getting close to Snowdon's summit in April 2018, with Wyn standing by to support me in case I slipped.

Returning to Helena Ward to see the amazing nurses and physiotherapists who helped me on my journey to recovery.

Feeling on top of the world after being able to walk down the aisle unaided to marry Lois in Italy.

Standing at the peak of Mont Buet with my stepmum, Sue, almost 18 months after my accident.

Me and Lois with the welcoming party who greeted us off the airplane in Nepal, outside the spinal unit in Kathmandu.

The view of Mount Everest from the top of Mera Peak, Nepal.

Proud to have reached the summit of Mera Peak with Bigraj, Rich, Doc and Millimetres 2 Mountains supporters in November 2019.

to make it through to 30 without retiring from injuries. If you made it past that ripe old age, then you would retire around 34 because you couldn't keep up with the new kids on the block.

Since my mid-twenties, I knew I had to find something else to do for the rest of my working life. I'd always had other interests and never let rugby define me. Too many people hang their hat on their profession. Take it away, and they struggle to know what's left.

Also, rugby players are not paid like football players. Yes, we earn a decent salary whilst we can still play, but we don't earn in a week what the average Joe would earn in a year like a lot of football players do. Therefore, I couldn't kick my heels up and wax on about my glory days to anyone who'd listen for the rest of my life. I had to find a way to earn a living. I was registered as disabled and couldn't walk. My options were somewhat limited, and I'd probably have to give up that childhood dream of working with the tigers at Longleat Safari Park, but I had some options and I had a feeling that more would come.

There was no rush for the moment, but I knew that it was something I would have to mull over during the coming months.

I wanted to work; I just needed to figure out where.

CHAPTER 12

NEW YORK, NEW YORK!

Humming Frank Sinatra's song to myself, I looked out of the window as Pete pulled up on his Vespa. It was a warm summer's evening, nearly two weeks since my release from hospital and we had fallen into an easy routine. I had settled into a twelve-hour day of rehab, either working with a physio or by myself. Pete would come over several times a week for sessions and I would visit the physio clinic where Kim worked on the alternating days.

I had also started seeing an occupational therapist about my left hand. If I was honest with myself, I had probably been neglecting it. My fingers curled in and I had lost most of my strength. It's easy to forget about the smaller things when you're trying to learn to walk again.

Wheeling myself over to the top of the stairs, I pressed the intercom to let Pete in. A few seconds later, his head popped around the bottom of the steps with the unmistakable Ferrari logo on the front of his baseball cap.

'Pete . . . do you only buy Italian products?'

He nodded and then cleared his throat.

'Fair enough,' I said.

At least I had a good idea of what to get him for Christmas.

'How's it going with the crutches?' he asked.

I'd been practising for the last week and was now able to stumble around the house with them.

'I'm still struggling to straighten my left leg. It looks like I'm a cartoon character trying to creep up on someone.'

As amusing as my left leg's antics were, they needed to stop so that I didn't pick up too many bad habits, or give someone a heart attack.

'We can take a look at it this evening,' Pete said. 'I've got something that might help with your foot drop as well . . .'

Two hours later, Pete was on his way out and my friend, Rich, who went to school with me and Tom, helped get me ready for a shower. With Lois away, Rich had moved in to perform the role of my 1950s housewife. He would cook, help get me dressed and undressed, pass anything I couldn't reach, ferry me to hospital appointments and even wash my hair – things only a best friend could do without me feeling awkward about it. In return, I let him have a go on my wheelchair whenever he wanted.

As he pulled a T-shirt over my head, I caught sight of his tattoo of Russian lettering that read 'Brothers in Arms' – the same one as I have on my forearm. It had been Tom's idea. For years he'd bugged us both to get it done. We had refused, laughing it off as another one of Tom's crazy ideas. I wasn't really a tattoo person and thought Tom would let it rest, but he never did. Shortly after Tom's death, Rich and I had got the tattoos Tom had always wanted. I wish we'd done it earlier.

'You know,' I said, as Rich put my T-shirt in the laundry basket, 'the three of us haven't exactly had the best run . . .'

'You two maybe,' Rich responded, as he got a clean T-shirt out of my drawer. 'I'm all right. Not even a broken toe.'

'You know what Tom would say right now?' I mused, sitting on the edge of my bed.

Rich held up one of my T-shirts. 'He'd ask why you have a *Jurassic Park* T-shirt with "Raptor Trainer" on it?'

'Stag do. Anyway, Tom would say that he wouldn't want to be you right now.' I grinned at him. 'There were three of us. Tom died, I broke my neck; what's going to happen to you?'

Rich rolled his eyes.

'I'm just saying that if this was a film, you'd be screwed.'

Rich laughed. 'Like in that film *Final Destination*?'

'Exactly. I've had my accident and survived, so you're next.'

Rich started patting his pockets.

'I think I left my phone in the living room,' he said. 'I'll just go and get it.'

'Mind the stairs!' I called out after him.

Lois had returned from New Zealand with half the chocolate supply of the Southern Hemisphere and, with her return, I felt that another piece of my life had slotted back into place.

A week later we were off to a friend's wedding. I had missed a lot while I had been in hospital. Through social media I had watched as holidays, stag dos, birthdays and weddings passed by without me. This was the first social event that I'd sworn to myself that I would attend.

A weekend away was a daunting prospect and required some stringent planning. We had spent three days laying out everything I'd need. My days of chucking some pants and a toothbrush into a rucksack had firmly passed. Lois and I had talked through various scenarios and how we would deal with them. It was fear of the unknown that made us nervous. Simple things such as a narrow doorway needed consideration. I was most worried about my catheter slipping. I knew everyone would laugh it off, but if the truth be told I'd rather not wet myself during the wedding ceremony.

Fortunately, this didn't happen and the weekend went well with only one hiccup. I had managed to drop the power unit for my FES machine, that lifted my foot, down the toilet. It was therefore a wheelchair for me until the bride's father managed to dry it out overnight in an airing cupboard. Everyone had made me feel welcome; no one mollycoddled me or made a point of singling me out. My rugby friends had treated me as if nothing had changed. They made me join them on the dancefloor in my wheelchair, never let me have an empty glass and took great pleasure in making me explain in detail the more explicit side to hospital life – the more intimate, the better. I had relaxed, joined in with the celebrations, drunk perhaps a bit too much and generally enjoyed myself.

The next day, waving goodbye to the other guests, Lois pulled out of the driveway. Out of nowhere, I burst into tears. I was sobbing so much that Lois had to pull the car over to check on me.

'What's wrong, Ed?' she asked, leaning over. 'I thought you had a great time.'

I smiled at her through the sheet of water that now covered most of my face.

'Nothing's wrong.' I gulped, trying to calm my breathing. 'It's just there were so many times in the hospital when I wondered whether I'd be able to enjoy a weekend like this. I thought I'd never do this again . . .'

Lois leant over and hugged me. 'I thought those days might be over for us too.'

I straightened and wiped my face with my sleeve. 'Sorry

about that, I don't know what came over me. Normal service has resumed. McDonald's immediately.'

She smiled at me before starting up the engine.

It was a few minutes before I spoke again.

'If we can attend someone else's wedding . . . then why don't we attend our own?'

Lois stared at me. 'Do you think you could do it? We were going to be in Italy for two weeks.'

I nudged her arm. 'Eyes on the road, please. And yes, I don't see why not. We'll just have to leave six weeks free to pack everything . . .'

I smiled at the woman I'd hopefully be marrying in a year's time.

I had attended my first wedding since the accident, and got through it, and the following weekend I went to my first rugby match, to see my old team, the Dragons, play rugby in Wales. I wasn't just watching this one either; I'd been told in advance that I would be interviewed down on the pitch and hosted in the President's box – the full five-star treatment.

Peering down at my former teammates from the best seats in the stadium, I watched as they ran onto the pitch. I was excited about seeing them back in action. I'd already popped into the changing rooms before the match and had wished them all luck. As they took to the pitch, the roar of the crowd was deafening and the atmosphere electrifying. A wave of sadness rolled over me. I would never experience that moment again of trotting out in front of a crowd of thousands. I would never be part of a professional sports team again. I was going to miss that.

The moment was only fleeting. I wouldn't let it linger and ruin the rest of the game for me. All things come to an end and often quite abruptly. That's life, and I was okay with it.

I'd had a decade playing a game that I loved with some great memories and, even more importantly, some great mates. Two things that couldn't be taken away from me.

Lois nudged me and pointed up at the large screen at one end of the stadium. 'Look, it's you!'

I glanced up. Taking up the entirety of it was my slightly gormless face. At least nothing close to regret had passed across my features in that moment – I'd take gormless anytime over that. I gave a wide grin and a wave, but the cameraman had already moved on to someone else.

If you ever want to feel like a celebrity, I recommend turning up at Heathrow Airport in a wheelchair with a catheter bag hanging off the side. Queues evaporate, side doors open and luggage is magicked to its destination.

The consultant had given me the all-clear, and Lois and I had been packing for a week – we were off to New York. Yes, travelling to another continent less than four months after having nearly severed your spinal cord is not what most would do, but I wanted to live again. Fortunately, I was now able to walk a bit with my crutches so had decided to use these during the night and a wheelchair during the day.

When I'd first been given the tickets to see Fleetwood Mac, the overriding feeling I had was fear. How hard was it going to be? What if I had an accident over there? What if they wouldn't let me fly? It was fear of the unknown again. It had to be beaten into submission every day or I wouldn't recover the life that I wanted.

As Dad unloaded our suitcases from the back of his car, I stared up at the huge glass doors of the airport from my wheelchair. I swallowed. Maybe this was too much . . .

Lois came up behind me, obviously sensing my nervousness. 'What did we say our mantra was?'

'Just go for it,' I responded, smiling up at her.

We had spent weeks planning and I knew we couldn't have done any more to prepare for it.

We'd only been in the airport for a few minutes when we were swept off by the staff who looked after everything for us. The same level of care and service continued throughout the flight and our arrival at JFK airport. Leaving the slick, air-conditioned building, the full blast of sweltering New York sunshine signalled that we were on our own. We ordered our Uber and waited for a larger one that could accommodate my wheelchair and got going.

Fortunately, my celebrity position was reinstated the next day when we arrived to see Fleetwood Mac at Citi Field – concert arena by night and baseball park by day. Without any delay, I was ushered to the wheelchair section of the front row, right in front of the metal railings. Some people had been waiting hours to get one of these coveted positions. I felt like we had queue jumped, but I consoled myself that I had to find some perks in not being able to walk or pee by myself. Lois and I took up our positions and waited. This was easier for me as I was in my wheelchair, while Lois had to stand for what felt like hours. The crowds swarmed and the sense of anticipation was palpable. The throb of weaving voices swelled before erupting into cheers as the band took to the stage.

They opened with 'The Chain' and I couldn't have been happier. The band moved effortlessly from hit to hit and the crowd was whipped into a frenzy. When 'Everywhere' came on, I pushed myself up, balanced against the railing and bobbed my top half along with everyone else. Glancing back at the crowd of thousands, I thought of how lucky I was to be experiencing life again and all the technicolour joy it could bring. Catching some of the strange looks people were giving me, I realised they must have thought my standing up was a miracle induced by the power of Fleetwood Mac. Or that I was some fraudster who blagged all the best tickets with the help of his prop wheelchair.

It was official – I was now a fanboy of a band who were old enough to be my grandparents. With the encore, fireworks were set off around the stadium, and Lois and I hugged as we watched them in the warmth of the summer evening.

A day into our trip, Lois and I had to adapt our initial plans to travel around the city via cab. An Uber was never more than three minutes away and the SUVs had plenty of room in their trunks for my wheelchair. However, they're pretty expensive and the traffic in Manhattan is so bad that we were spending half our tourist-time trapped inside a stationary car, peeling our damp legs off fake-leather interiors. I could walk a bit on my crutches but not enough to last a full day out so I still needed my wheelchair with me. From my experience of previous trips to New York, I knew that the subway was the quickest way around. Half of the stations were wheelchair accessible, and these had lifts and were spread evenly over the city.

As I rolled up to the station marked on my map as having a lift, Lois and I stared at each other. It was now or never.

'What did we say our mantra was?' Lois said, a little less confidently than at the airport.

'Just go for it!' I replied, trying to keep the enthusiasm clear in my voice although I wasn't feeling it.

One stinky elevator ride later, we found our way onto a subway train hurtling underground in the depths of the city. Getting on the train had been fine. We let a couple of them pass so we could find a position on the platform where the lip of the train doors almost touched the platform. I then flicked the front wheels of my wheelchair over the lip when the next train arrived. People parted to make room for us and a few smiled at me.

Lois and I exchanged glances as we counted down the stops. We were playing 'platform gap roulette' and, as the doors at our station slid open, we realised that we'd lost. A huge chasm was in front of us. The only way I'd get my wheelchair to the other side was if I had a thirty-metre run-up and pole vault. Added to this was the fact there was a timer on the doors that was beeping its impatience.

Hauling myself to my feet, I lined up my crutches and turned to the man standing next to me. I then did something I was still getting used to.

'Can you help us, please?' I asked.

'Sure thing, buddy,' he said, as he grabbed my wheelchair and lifted it onto the platform.

Lois took my arm and helped me take the large stride required.

The man then hopped back onto the train just as the doors were closing.

'Thank you!' we both shouted as I settled back into my wheelchair.

As I was waving a crutch at the departing train, I realised that the idea of using the subway was much scarier than the reality.

This was the thing about New York. It defied our expectations again and again. The kindness of busy city dwellers was abundant. Many people would offer their help in a calm, polite manner. On the few occasions people didn't because they had their heads buried in a newspaper or eyes closed in half-sleep, I only had to ask for it. The vast majority went out of their way to help me and Lois with a smile and a wave. I am a firm believer that there is more good in people than we give them credit for.

That Saturday night I was in New York, shuffling around a hotel lobby on my crutches with a jovial smile and a slightly drunk Lois, celebrating our last night in the Big Apple. By Monday morning, I was back in Salisbury Hospital for an appointment about my catheter. It should have been a bump back to Earth, but actually both were equally exciting. I'd finally been given the news that I had been waiting for – my catheter could come out. The source of most of my medical issues since the accident would be gone. Eight tubes, three urinary tract infections, two cystoscopies, one false passage and a flesh wound, all in the space of four months. Good riddance to it.

I now had the challenge of retraining my bladder to full fitness as it had forgotten a lot of what it had learnt during my adult life. I would therefore have to keep myself close to a toilet at all times over the next few weeks. I would happily risk a few accidents in exchange for a functional bladder. Like most things, I had to put in the effort to reap the rewards.

When I opened the door to the waiting room, Lois looked up at me from her chair. 'The wedding venue has just emailed. They'd saved our original date, even though we'd cancelled. We can still get married there!'

I offered her my arm. We had some planning to do.

CHAPTER 13

THE ONLY WAY IS UP . . .

'You're making me nervous,' Pete said, staring up at me.

'Come on now. You were the one who suggested that we try some hill climbing.'

'I said "in a few weeks' time",' Pete responded. 'It's only been a day since I said that.'

'At least it's Monday, so technically it's next week.' Pete shifted his weight between his legs and I buckled. 'Okay, how about just some uneven ground this week, and if it all goes well, a bit of a slope next week.'

'Deal,' Pete said. 'And you're putting the harness on.'

Wyn bent down to dig around in the oversized bag he carried everywhere, before producing what looked like toddler reins.

'Deal,' I responded.

Wyn looped the reins around my waist and took the end of them. He was a big guy and the idea was that if I stumbled he would either keep me upright or help reduce the speed at which I fell.

It was four months after my accident and we were standing at the edge of a local field. I had two walking poles for support that worked in a similar way to crutches and two pretty amazing physios as backup. I couldn't have been better equipped. Taking my first steps, I realised that walking on uneven ground would not only be a physical strain but a mental one too. Every step had to be considered for both foot placement and timing of the FES machine. The weakness in my left-side core muscles also made my left leg wobblier, so I walked better with the help of a crutch, walking pole, or a hand. The main problem was that my left foot didn't lift very high, so the risk of tripping was always present.

The point of this new exercise was not only to get those reluctant muscles working again, but to also start firing up the neurological messages from my brain. When you put yourself in a precarious situation your brain works overtime, shooting messages to different areas of your body – preparing you to fight off danger, or run away from it. I needed those messages to start reaching their destinations, so even a walk over an uneven field was helping my neurological recovery. I had a goal in mind: I wanted to be able to walk down the aisle at my wedding without using a crutch or walking pole.

An hour later, after a large circle of the field, we decided that I'd done enough. I checked the distance tracker on my watch – 500 metres. It didn't sound like much but I put it into context. Two months ago, I couldn't even take a step without Lois lifting my foot for me.

Later that week, I had an appointment with Mr Barua, the spinal surgeon who had saved my life at Southmead Hospital. As I'd made my way past Costa Coffee in the hospital foyer, I smiled as I imagined myself lying in my hospital bed sucking a frothy coffee through a straw. Things were different this time; no one paid any attention to a man walking through a hospital foyer with a crutch. I hadn't been stared at and it had felt great.

When I entered Mr Barua's office using only one crutch, his expression momentarily revealed his shock but he quickly recovered.

'Well, I've got to be honest, I never expected this!'

I had thought about this moment for hours. What do you say to someone whom you don't really know, but owe your life to? In the end I hadn't said very much. I had thanked him profusely, of course, and was quite pleased with myself for not trying to hug him. But when I'd got home I thought that perhaps it hadn't been enough, so I'd tapped out a post on Instagram about my visit:

Seeing his reaction today really made me realise just how lucky I got and how close I was to this being a completely different story. Neil, if you're reading this I couldn't really articulate it earlier but thank you . . . thank you for making the decision to operate immediately, thank you for being so good at your job and most of all thank you for giving me a fighting chance.

Ever since I was discharged from hospital, I knew there was somewhere else I had to visit.

It was a bright sunny day as I stopped for a moment to steady myself at the bottom of the stone steps that led down to the pool. The only sound was the rippling surface that swirled out from the water feature. I'd already taken my FES machine off at the house and, with the aid of both crutches, I made the final shuffle to the edge of the pool. Balancing my weight, I tried to tug my feet out of my unlaced trainers. The right one came out smoothly but I couldn't lift my left leg high enough to free the foot from my trainer. Persevering with it, I repeated the action but I still couldn't get the angle right.

'Shall I get that for you?' Lois asked.

I nodded.

With no further comment and minimum fuss, Lois leant down and pulled my already unlaced trainer off. Next was my shirt. Balancing on my left crutch, I undid the buttons down the middle with my right hand and pulled out each arm in turn. In my first month at home, I had quickly learnt not to bother doing up cuff buttons on my shirts if I could get away with it – I struggled to undo the buttons of my right sleeve as my left hand didn't have the dexterity to deal with them.

Lowering myself to the ground, I landed heavily and with little grace. I unhooked my arms from my crutches and slid them along the side of the pool. Supporting my weight with my arms I leant to the right as I lowered my body into the shallow end of the pool. The water lapped gently against my chest but I could only feel it in certain areas.

I was back in the pool where I had broken my neck. A ten-second event that had taken me from the bottom of the stone steps, shedding my shirt and shoes on the way, to diving in.

Walking further into the deeper end, I appreciated the ease of movement that came with the buoyancy of the water. There was no fear or worry about the pool. My diving days were over anyway – the pool would have to try a lot harder if it wanted to finish me off.

Lying on the carpet, I took a moment to catch my breath. My shoulder ached and my face was only inches from the sharp point of the coffee table. After gingerly testing that everything was still working, I stared up at the white ceiling.

I'd had another fall.

This was something I was having to get used to after deciding not to use my wheelchair in the house any more. My leg would go into spasm, or sometimes it was poor timing on my FES machine lifting my foot. Often it was just a general lack of balance. Any of these things could send me tumbling to the ground. I'd go into shock for a few seconds and then have to try to roll myself into a position where I could pull myself up. So far, I hadn't done much damage beyond some cracking bruises. I'd quickly learnt to always look for somewhere safe and furniture-free to angle myself towards in case I fell.

It was the feeling of being accelerated into my eighties that got me down. I had to be careful all the time and consider where I was placing my feet. I couldn't allow myself to be distracted by anything as I moved around the rooms in my dad's house. A simple conversation could send me tumbling to the ground. I was too young for this.

Rubbing my shoulder, I used the couch to pull myself up. I was now late calling the wife of a man who had recently sustained a spinal cord injury. She had contacted me through Instagram and I'd promised that I'd talk her through what she and her husband were facing. This was the first time I had offered to do this. I wasn't really sure what to say, I guessed that a large part of it was just to listen. I still clearly remembered all of the confusion and anxiety my family and I went through in the early days of my own injury.

'I just don't know what I should be doing to help him,' she

said after she had explained the details of her husband's injuries and treatment so far. It was strange to hear about someone else's story, so similar to my own.

I thought about it carefully before I spoke. 'It sounds like you are doing loads to support him. Just being at hospital with him will help more than you can imagine.'

'But there must be something more I can do . . .' she said.

Was this how it had been for Lois all those weeks I was in hospital? Back then, just her presence had been enough to reassure me, but she'd been desperate to find something practical she could do to help. Maybe that's what the relatives need in these situations.

I took a breath. 'Let's talk about the steps to move him from intensive care to a spinal injury ward, because then he can start physio. That transfer is something you can possibly try and help speed up . . .'

Two hours later, with promises to call again later in the week, I turned off my phone. I was in exactly the same position on the couch as I had been when I'd made the call, but my mental outlook had shifted. The transformation was huge. No longer did I feel aggrieved with my situation; it had been replaced by a calmness and a degree of perspective. Settling back into the cushions, I realised that I'd had my first taste of the power of helping others. Of course I would still have called her next week even if this call had made me miserable afterwards, but it hadn't; the bonus was that I felt grounded and able to tackle anything that was presented to me.

I had been thinking about this for the last few days. Having spent quite a bit of time by myself in recent weeks, I'd had time to reflect on lasting happiness. What had become apparent to me was that happiness was like a cup: some things I put into it would quickly evaporate; but others would keep that cup filled for much longer. I'd even started making lists of what had longer-lasting effects, marking them from one to ten. One meant there was an instantaneous high that faded within a few minutes and ten lasted several days. Here's what I came up with:

- Helping others: 10
- Seeing friends: 9
- Walk with just me and the dogs: 8
- Spontaneous hug from Lois: 7 (rugby lads, admit it – men need hugs too)
- Beating my own time at something: 6 (rewarding, yet never-ending)
- Completing a task I had been putting off for days: 5
- New toy, gadget, present to myself: 4 (the anticipation of owning it was often more exciting)
- Beating someone else's time at something: 3 (instantly rewarding, but there is always someone better than you)
- Takeaways: 2 (sometimes, when this was particularly ineffective, I would start planning my next takeaway while eating the current one)
- Video games: 1 (fun at the time but no real happiness left over. Sometimes this is -1 when I lose badly)

Writing out this list made me realise that I needed to move away from the bottom four. The amount of time or money I put into them didn't produce the rewards that came from the top six. I'd learnt a long time ago, when Tom had died, that life can be very short, and that happiness is something that needs to be worked at.

Over time, I had started to get used to my situation. However, occasionally, something still caught me off guard and made me step outside myself for a moment. Attending a fundraising curry night for my rehab was one of them. Who would have thought I'd end up in this position? That people would care enough to donate to the causes that I supported.

Early on in my recovery, when the charity Restart had become involved, I had made a promise that I would pay back every single penny that was donated to my rehab. I wanted them to be able to pass the funds on to others who needed them just as much as I had.

Holding Lois's hand, I entered the restaurant in Bath where the fundraiser was being held. Although very grateful that it had been organised, I was struggling with the idea of it as I didn't think I had done anything to deserve it. The room was packed and there was a small cheer when I popped my head around the door to the function room. I spotted a few familiar faces but also a lot of people I had never met before. I spent the first hour trying to make my way around everyone to thank them for turning up. I was a bit overwhelmed. We all sat down for a meal, and I answered everyone's questions before some live music started up. Here I was, the recipient of so many good wishes and pats on the back (not to mention the generous donations that I could pass on to Restart). It made my head spin.

This is what I want to do. This is what I want to work on.

I'd had an epiphany. The most rewarding thing I'd done since my accident was speaking to other spinal cord patients and their families, helping them face what was probably one of the toughest curveballs they had ever been dealt.

How could I scale this up? The best way would be to help raise money for others who needed it most. The more I raised, the more people I could help. I just didn't know where to start or how I would fit it in with trying to get back to work. These questions were hardly the 'finer details', but they could wait for the moment. At least I had a goal, an outline of what my future could be.

The following day I tapped out a message on Instagram.

I've been to my fair share of fundraisers in the past, that's nothing new, but how the hell have I become the benefactor of one?! It's crazy but it's also lucky. I probably use the word lucky too much and should consult a thesaurus now and again but it's the best way to describe how I feel most of the time. I'm not saying that it's all down to random chance, what I really mean is that I'm fortunate (lucky) that I have the means to at least have a chance of a decent recovery and Monday night was just an example of that. At the same time, I'm fully aware that many others aren't afforded the same opportunities that I am. This has become increasingly clear to me having got to know so many others with SCIs over the last few months and is something I am determined to shed more light on and try and change moving forward.
watch this space

I'd put my intention out there, in front of thousands of people. I couldn't go back now.

CHAPTER 14

NEW CHAPTER

I watched as Lois cooked for us. Bringing the spoon to her mouth, she considered the sauce for a moment before adding a sprinkle of this and a dash of that. She was able to make a mouth-watering dish from any ingredients presented to her. Whenever I cooked, I'd chuck everything into a pan, cross my fingers and top up everyone's wine glasses if it didn't come out as expected.

'So, I saw Alex today,' I said, trying to fill the silence.

'Oh, yeah,' she responded, not looking up at me. 'How's he doing?'

I rattled off a few of Alex's anecdotes, all the time watching Lois. Not once had she looked up at me.

Silence descended on us again.

'Can I do anything to help?' I asked for the third time.

'No, just sit there. I'm nearly done now.'

Lois pulled cutlery out of the drawer and walked out to the terrace to set the table . . . I could have done that. I followed her outside and took a seat, trying to think of topics to get her to talk to me.

It was late when we finished dinner, nearly nine thirty, as I had been working on my physio until eight.

'Right, that's me done for the day,' Lois said, already pushing her chair away from the table and picking up our plates. 'I'm going to get an early night. Try not to wake me when you come in.'

I watched as she retreated inside the house.

Things hadn't been great the last two days, but everything had been brilliant up until then. It had been three months since I'd left hospital, my recovery was going really well, Lois had been incredibly supportive and we'd been seeing all our friends again. I'd thought that everything was back to normal.

I wracked my brain. What could be upsetting her? Perhaps she was missing work. She hadn't gone back yet as I was still waiting for the DVLA to agree to me driving an automatic car. In the meantime, Lois therefore had to ferry me to all my appointments. My licence should be coming through the following month and then she could return to work. It must be that . . .

An hour later, I got undressed outside the bedroom, hoping not to wake her. When I entered the room she was silent, but I knew she wasn't asleep. Climbing into bed, I reached down with my hands and pulled my left leg underneath the covers. Lying on my back, I stared up at the ceiling in the dark. Two people awake but pretending to be asleep. There was an ocean between us.

The next morning Lois disappeared for three hours. I was busy with Pete, but I had seen her car leave. She hadn't said goodbye, which wasn't like her. She was probably just going to see a friend and hadn't mentioned it. I tried to distract myself with my physio and avoided thinking about where she was. She needed her freedom just as much as I did. I couldn't wait to get my driving licence again, to be able to head out whenever I wanted and in whichever direction I chose.

It must be really tough for her being tied to the house, I thought, waiting for when I need her.

After lunch, Lois's car pulled up and our two dogs barked their greetings. They scampered down the stairs to meet her, but I remained where I was – by the time I negotiated getting down the stairs, she would be halfway up them.

When her head popped up above the staircase, I looked down at my iPad, not wanting to stare at her.

'I chased up the DVLA again,' I called out, my ears pricked, waiting for her answer.

She came straight over and sat on the coffee table in front of me.

'Ed, we need to talk.'

Crap. I went cold as I registered her tone. Something was very wrong.

'I went to see a therapist today,' Lois continued.

She couldn't meet my eyes as she spoke.

'Oh,' I said, blinking rapidly. 'So, it's not about my driving licence then?'

'What?'

'I thought you'd been quiet because you wanted to get back to work and needed me to get my driving licence.'

'No, no. It's not that.'

'Then, what? What's wrong?'

I leant forwards, waiting to hear if she had started feeling low, not quite herself and what I could do to help. It was really common for people who had sustained life-changing injuries to become depressed, and also those closest to them as well.

Lois started twisting her engagement ring rapidly. 'I went to see the therapist about us. I've had some worries for a while.'

I felt as if I'd been punched in the stomach. The air left me and I just stared at her. This couldn't be right; we were fine. Strongest couple around. Everyone said so.

'I'm sorry,' she said. 'There's a few things I need to talk to you about. The therapist said I had to be more honest with you.'

Oh, God. She hadn't . . . she couldn't . . . when would she even get the time? She was always here . . . although she had disappeared for a few hours last week.

I slumped back into the sofa. 'Who? How long . . .?'

'Oh, no, Ed!' Lois said, leaning forwards. 'It's nothing like that. I wouldn't do that, you know I wouldn't. Well, that's part of the problem actually . . .'

'Wait a second,' I said, my head spinning. 'Can we just be clear about this. You're not having an affair? And part of the problem is that you can't have one?'

She looked shocked, genuinely shocked.

I lowered my voice. 'Can you please just tell me what this is about?'

'Sorry, yes. I'm not doing very well at this . . . It's just that we've been together for years, spent most of our twenties as a couple. Grown up together, I suppose. We trained together, socialised together. We were busy all the time, a really tight couple, but also very independent of each other. It just worked . . . And it doesn't feel like that any more. I suppose we were a happy-go-lucky couple. And we weren't equipped to deal with this sort of thing.'

I nodded, trying to distract myself from wondering what the giant 'but' would be. 'Things will get better Lois; we'll get back to how we were before.'

She stared up at me. 'That's the thing, Ed. I don't think they will. This accident has altered you in so many ways. I don't even think you're aware of them.'

I tried not to react but inside I was crumbling. Was I so different? Had I not noticed something that everyone else was aware of?

'So, you've been feeling like this right since day one?' I asked. 'Right from when I was lying in that hospital bed?'

'Not right after the accident. In the first couple of months I went into "Monster Mode". I tried to become superhuman, was all over everything, trying to be there for you every minute of the day. I arranged everything that we needed, kept our house going, kept you going when you were down. I was just so grateful that you were alive. And then I was so proud of you for throwing everything into your recovery. You were amazing.'

'But . . .'

'But now you've been out of hospital for three months and I don't think it's going to go back to how it was before. It's like I'm having to get used to being engaged to a different man. The accident changed you. Not in a bad way. You're just . . . different. Everyone thinks we've returned to a normal life, but it's not normal for us.'

My heart began to hammer in my chest as I scrabbled to understand what she was saying. I couldn't be that different . . . could I?

'How have I changed?'

'Your priorities have changed. You don't have the personal ambition for yourself career wise . . . You've started getting really into charity work now. Which I'm proud of you for, but you don't seem to know what you want for yourself. Rugby used to take up so much of your time and that has just gone.'

I hadn't realised that those things were so important to her.

'You can't be upset at me for wanting to do charity work?'

'No, of course I'm not. I think it's great you want to do it.

You're just so preoccupied with it . . . you're so *serious* about it. And between that and your rehab, it doesn't leave much room for anything else. I don't want you to change that; it's just something I'm going to have to get used to.'

I took a moment before daring to ask my next question. 'Are there other ways I've changed?'

Lois swallowed and dipped her head. 'Physically you've changed. You've lost loads of weight, which was so sad to see. I know it sounds really shallow, but it was who you were. You worked so hard to get to a place where you were confident with your body.'

These were the words I had feared the most. I'd known that I wasn't the big, strapping rugby player any more. But to hear her say this hurt more than I'd imagined. My chest felt tight as I realised that she was no longer attracted to me.

It was true, I had changed physically. Lying on my back for the best part of two months had meant I'd lost all that muscle. I couldn't get it back either; I didn't have the strength to work out in that way. I couldn't change back to the man I had been. What did that mean for us?

I took a deep breath. 'Do you not find me attractive any more?'

Tears formed in Lois's eyes. 'Yes, of course I do. I still find you attractive; you just look different, even smell different . . .'

'I smell different?' My cheeks burned. 'Lois, do I smell?'

The shame. All this time and no one had told me . . .

'You don't smell in that way; you just smell different. Not like the man I was with for seven years. Oh God, I've made it all sound so negative. I didn't mean for it to come out that way. The accident showed me how much I love you. How strong our bond is. I just need to find a way to get used to the new Ed.'

Lois suddenly looked deflated, like all her energy had drained away.

'The therapist said that smell is really important to people,' she continued, speaking softly. 'That it contains all these memories about a person and if that changes, it takes a while to get used to someone again.'

'I'm sorry you've been feeling that way,' I said, leaning towards her, wanting to comfort her but not sure how.

'I've been finding it hard when we . . . you know,' she said, not meeting my eye.

I hadn't known. Sure, it wasn't quite the same. You don't sever eight millimetres of your spinal cord and take up swinging from the chandeliers again. We'd both been keen to get that side of our relationship back after I got out of hospital. The little blue pills had helped at first when the messages weren't going in the right direction and I'd spoken to other patients about it. We had been trying, and I thought it was going well . . . I'd obviously been wrong. I'd let her down, and I hadn't even noticed.

'Oh, God,' she said, dropping her head into her hands. 'I can't believe I'm even saying all of this to you . . .'

I reached for her and she didn't move away.

'I still love you,' she said. 'I still want to be with you. It's just that I'm having to get used to the new you. And when we're together, I feel like I'm cheating on the old Ed.'

I paused for a moment, before pulling her into my arms. She didn't resist and curled up against me. 'So that's why you said it would be easier if you were the type of person who could have an affair?'

She nodded.

If it was possible, I loved her twice as much in that

moment. I hadn't realised the lengths she had been going to, just to make me feel wanted. All that time she hadn't felt comfortable with me. The enormity of what she had done was inescapable.

'I'm so sorry, Lois. I'm so sorry I didn't realise. I was so busy trying to tick off a list of everything I could do again, that I didn't notice how it was affecting you.'

Lois sniffed and wiped her eyes. 'I do still love you. And I'm sorry it's taking me longer than I thought. I'm so proud of you and everything you've done.'

'We'll take it very slowly. Go right back to basics. No pressure, no expectations. We'll take it at your speed.'

She looked up at me. 'And you're okay with that?'

'Of course I am. The last thing I want is for you to be uncomfortable with anything. Why would I ever want that?'

She smiled at me. 'Thank you. The therapist has made a few suggestions. She was really helpful, actually.'

I kissed her forehead, and we talked, curled up together, for the rest of the afternoon.

I had never been one to talk about my feelings, and neither had Lois. We just got on with things and tried to find the fun side to life. I suppose that's where we were tested – there's limited fun to be found in relearning the things you first conquered when you were 2 years old, or watching the man you love change beyond recognition. We did it, though; we tried to make the daily tasks as light-hearted and interesting as we could. But that light-heartedness couldn't fix everything. Not everything can be made better with a joke. We needed to be able to talk to each other when we couldn't deal with something by ourselves.

'Do you know,' Lois said, as she got up to close the curtains against the night sky, 'this is the lightest I've felt in months. Just being honest with you has taken this weight away from me.'

I watched her as she moved freely around the room. 'I didn't know. I hadn't the slightest clue that you were keeping everything inside. You were always so cheerful.'

'I suppose I felt it was my duty to do that. You had enough going on without me adding to it.' She held her hand out to me. 'But no more secrets.'

I needed to test myself. The urge had been with me for a month and, with Pete's blessing, Lois, Wyn and a few friends joined me for my first hill climb. We had chosen the Blorenge peak in Wales as we could park a car at the top and I wouldn't have to walk back down again. I had also hiked it the year before, so it was a good benchmark for what I was capable of before and after my injury.

It was nearly eight months since my accident and I had so far only walked uphill for one mile on tarmac. I was really going to test myself by walking four miles this time.

Wyn was by my side as I set off with two walking poles to steady myself on the steep woodland ground. It was late November and the russet golds and reds of the leaves high up in the trees were a dangerous distraction. Keeping my eyes firmly fixed on the ground, I navigated my way around fallen branches and protruding rocks. Fifty steps in, I realised that I'd thrown myself in at the deep end. With each step I had to tense my core to be able to lift my left leg high enough to clear the ground.

Lois and our friends walked ahead at a leisurely pace and

then sat for ten minutes while I picked my way around the various obstacles that woodland undergrowth brings with it. I tried not to think of all the walks we had been on together where I was always the first to the top, sometimes even jogging the last stretch to work on my cardio. The first half an hour was exhausting – step, tense, big step . . . step, tense, big step . . . My stomach muscles ached, and I was beginning to wonder how I could bow out of this with my pride still intact.

As I stopped for a moment to peer up the ascent, another walker was on his way down the hill. With no shame, he looked me up and down. I met his gaze, my walking poles in hand and the FES machine that lifted my foot on show.

'You'll struggle up there, mate,' he said, before briskly carrying on down the hill.

For some people that might have been confirmation that they should turn around. For me, it was the motivation I needed to keep going.

I put my head down and got back to it.

A year ago, I had romped up this hill in just over an hour. I'd jogged the last bit and then circled back round to chivvy along the other people we were with. I wasn't showing off (well, maybe a little) but I loved to push myself, test myself at all times.

The second time I tackled this hike I had certainly tested myself. What once took me just over sixty minutes, now took three and a half hours. Yet, instead of regretting my loss of movement, I basked in the knowledge that I'd made it to the top. I still had the mental strength to keep going, had managed not to damage myself and there was a great pub back at the bottom.

In the following days, we waited to see if there were any knock-on effects, but there weren't. I felt both physically and mentally alive. It may have been because I had given myself a few days of rest afterwards, but I believe this feeling of well-being came because I had achieved something. I had challenged myself and I'd won.

My birthday, Christmas and New Year passed in a flurry of celebrations but also some moments of quiet reflection. I had started giving some charity talks, which had taken my life in an interesting direction. A couple of times a month, I would be up on stage talking about topics that ranged from spinal injuries to long stays in hospital and enforced career changes. Surprisingly, I found that I could speak openly and honestly about my experiences without any negative emotions. Of course, it was unsettling at first to speak about personal issues in front of people I didn't know, but it soon became normal and I now had no issue standing up in front of four hundred people and explaining how catheters worked.

On the surface, I looked as though I had nearly made a full recovery. Yes, I used walking poles to get around and my gait was uneven, which created a limp. But on the whole, it looked like I was able to move around with relative ease. I was so grateful to be at this point in my recovery but a lot of it was smoke and mirrors. The truth was that if my FES stopped working when I was out and about, I was pretty much rendered immobile. This caused a lot of underlying stress and whenever I left the house I had to pack spare pads, units and batteries. There was also the issue of leg spasms – at my first talk I was nearly catapulted off the stage when all of the muscles in my left leg decided to randomly contract at the same time.

These things were frustrating; however, the most troublesome issue was still my bladder. I had been left with an overactive bladder that liked to spasm when it was asked to hold anything above 200ml. This meant I needed to use the toilet regularly and I had about two minutes before I couldn't hold it any longer. Whenever I went out I'd limit how much I drank and also relied on incontinence pads or pants – not something that this 29-year-old thought would become part of his morning routine, but it was better than the alternative. The pads rarely got called into action, but it was reassuring to know that if I did have an accident then it would be trickles rather than floods. If I had to go on a long journey or attend an event that would last several hours, I would wear a convene or 'condom catheter' which attaches to a 500ml leg bag. This could slip and explosions had been known to happen, so none of my options were foolproof, but, without them, I would be limited to staying within fifty metres of a toilet.

When I had been thinking about how my life would change in the long-term after the accident, I worried about lots of things – my relationships, whether I'd walk again – but never thought this would be one of them. I had believed it would resolve itself in a few months. Yet it's such a huge part of everyday life and affects so many people with spinal cord injuries, as well as a whole load of other medical reasons for incontinence. So many spinal cord injury patients have confided in me that this is the thing that affects them the most, so I really believe it's important we can talk about it.

Despite all of the difficulties with getting out, I wanted to keep going with my charity work and Lois was fully supportive of my wishes. We just had to figure out a way to scale it up.

Surrounded by boxes, Lois and I sipped our first glass of wine in our new home, a rented cottage up the hill from my dad. We hadn't gone far as our lives were here now. We loved Cardiff but had only moved there for my rugby contract and it was a long distance from the majority of our friends. We were incredibly grateful to my dad and Sue for putting up with us for six months, but it was the start of a new year and we wanted to move on with our lives.

Lois was curled up next to me on the sofa and there had been a comfortable silence as we watched the flames flicker in the open fire. She idly ran her hand along my arm as we sipped at our wine.

'I've been thinking, Lois.'

'Yes?'

'About how I can try and raise more money for charity.'

She pulled herself up and crossed her legs underneath her.

'I'm going to climb Snowdon.'

'Oh,' she said. 'When?'

'In three months' time, just before the one-year anniversary of my accident.'

I studied her, waiting for her response. I needed her to be behind this, behind me.

She kissed me lightly on the cheek. 'Well, you said you were going to walk again, and you did. Who says you can't do this too?'

CHAPTER 15

SNOW AND SUN

Rolling out of my bunk bed, I pulled back the curtain and surveyed the scene. Bright sunshine lit up the early morning sky and there wasn't a cloud in sight. I opened the window and took a deep breath of crisp mountain air.

The warmth of Lois's arms encircled my waist. 'It's perfect weather, isn't it?'

Nodding my agreement, I turned to face her. 'My only regret is that I didn't bring my shorts.'

She smiled. 'We can always do a DIY job on your trousers if it gets too hot for you. And anyway, you might need some more shorts when we go on holiday.'

It was a week before the anniversary of my accident and a week before our holiday to the Philippines, but first I had a mountain to climb.

After spending the past few days checking the weather reports, I was beyond pleased to see that the climb up Snowdon would be going ahead. The conditions in Wales, never mind the mountains, had been changing on a daily basis. It was only after peering out of the window that morning that we decided to leave my snow spikes back at our rented cottage for the day.

The past couple of months had been spent training and fundraising for this climb. I had set an initial target of raising £2,000 and, thanks to many generous donations, my sponsorship had swelled to £20,000. Now I just had to make it to the top.

We piled out of the rented house and made our way to the car park where the hike would begin. My friends and family had made the effort to join me for this climb and there were thirteen of us staying in the cottage. I had also put out a few messages on social media that there was an open invitation to join us if anyone wanted to. I hadn't expected many to answer that call.

Laughing and chatting amongst ourselves as we pulled our rucksacks from the cars, I spied a large group of around seventy people in the corner who must have been a coach party. Double-checking my Artificial Foot Orthotic was in place, I pulled out my walking poles and headed to the car park gates. I had stopped using my electric FES machine for the off-road hikes as it would often misjudge the timing of my steps. Instead, I now relied on a manual AFO that looped around my shin and shoe. As I limped across the tarmac, testing the newly applied straps on my ankle and knee, the coach party streamed towards me.

'Ed!' one of them called out.

I turned but didn't recognise him. He waved at me, as did some of the others.

It was then that I realised they weren't a coach party after all; they'd come here for me. I was incredibly humbled to see so many people whom I had never met before waiting to accompany me up the highest peak in England and Wales.

After I'd tried to introduce myself to as many of them as possible, they all looked at me expectantly.

I cleared my throat.

'Thank you all so much for choosing to spend your Saturday following me up a mountain. I really appreciate that you are taking time out of your busy lives. Nearly a year ago today, I broke my neck. I was told that it was unlikely that I would walk again and so it is important to me that I do this before the anniversary of my accident. I'm not just doing this to raise money for charity or to prove myself; I want to do this for everyone who has supported me during my recovery and for everyone who might use this as motivation in the future.'

There was a cheer from everyone around me.

'Oh, and one last thing,' I said, with a smile. 'Please go at your own pace, don't think that you have to hang back with me. I walk slowly and also need to stop every twenty minutes to pee. If I lag behind, don't worry . . . I'll see you at the top.'

With the rise of voices, everyone split off into smaller groups. I turned to Wyn and my friend Josh, who was a surgeon by day and a bodybuilder by night.

'Right, lads,' I said. 'Are we ready?'

'Ready when you are,' Wyn said, hoisting his ginormous bag onto his back.

Off we set, Wyn walking next to me and Josh behind. They were two of the biggest men I knew and were there to catch me if I fell. The sun was shining brightly and I had my family and friends here to support me – it didn't get much better than this. It was ten miles to get up Snowdon and back down again and I hadn't walked this far since my accident. It was unmapped territory and we were concerned that my left leg might give out.

With my trusty walking poles in both hands, we set off up the tarmacked road that formed the first mile of the hike. Tarmac is a relatively easy surface for me to walk on and, although steep, I was able to set off at a decent pace. It wasn't until we reached the proper path that I realised that I'd made a mistake. All the adrenaline buzzing around my body had made me walk too fast. I had committed the first sin of any endurance test; I'd forgotten that starting slower leads to finishing faster.

'Bloody hell,' I said, turning to face Wyn, 'I feel like I already need a lie down and a Mars bar.'

'Me too,' he said, adjusting the straps on his bag. 'The next section is a bit more uneven, so you'll naturally slow down. We'll adjust our pace.'

I began picking my way around the stones that were scattered across the steep hill. The group began to spread out as some of the fitter members surged on ahead whilst others dropped back and took their time. I felt a bit self-conscious as I was overtaken, but I knew that if I was going to make it to the top I was going to have to go at my own pace, one foot in front of the other, concentrating on every step.

Every few hundred metres I stopped staring at my feet for a moment to take in the view. The lush green landscape whipped up into the snowy peaks of the mountain range. Up ahead was the shallow tidal water of the Menai Strait that curled its way into the distance. This vast natural horizon stretched in front of me and my boundaries felt limitless.

Putting my head down again, I carried on for the next three miles, one foot in front of the other, my body beginning to ache with the strain.

Things began to get a bit more serious when we reached the snow line. By now a thick fog had descended onto the peak. Gone were the spectacular views and instead the world closed in on me. As we approached the last stop of the Snowdon mountain railway, I realised that the queue coming back down the mountain was impossibly long for this early in the day. Many of the hikers ahead of us must have been turning back before reaching the top.

Word spread down to me that the paths up ahead were treacherous with compacted snow and ice. The official advice had changed for the day – it was inadvisable to continue without crampons, long spikes that fit onto the bottom of your shoes. Stopping for a moment, I imagined my snow spikes sitting on the edge of my bunk bed back at the cottage; if only I could will them to appear in my bag. I'd decided to leave them behind as the weather had been so good.

Normally, I had difficulty stabilising myself on the uneven surface of a field; I took tumbles all the time. Add an ice rink into that equation, and things were starting to get pretty sketchy. With each step I took, it was pot luck whether my foot would slide from underneath me, with either Josh or Wyn needing to make a grab for me. Behind my big smiles and my best 'Bambi on Ice' impression, I was feeling nervous.

After my third muscle-jarring slip in under five minutes, my friend, Emily, approached us.

'I did bring these with me,' she said. 'I'm not sure if they'll fit you, but we could give them a go.'

She pulled a small set of snow spikes from her bag.

She crouched down and looped them around the bottom of both of my walking shoes. They were a bit tight but I tested them out for a few paces. They would give me a fighting chance.

The wind chill dropped to minus twelve degrees and we passed several of our party skidding their way back down to the train stop. They had to bow out with grace as they were wearing trainers. Without proper walking shoes for these conditions, they stood little chance of making it to the top.

On we climbed and the group thinned out even further. By now, I could only see a ten-metre circle around myself. My pace slowed when my hip began to tire. The studs on the bottom of my shoes were making it almost impossible for me to lift my foot high enough to clear the next step. The howling winds whipped around me, battering me from both sides, threatening to push me off balance.

I had to keep going; turning back wasn't an option now as the route down would be just as fraught.

There was no clever technique that we could think of to get me to the top; all I could do was rest my weight on my right leg and walking poles and slide my left leg all the way. Even though I was wearing only a T-shirt, the sweat was pouring down my face.

After another couple of hundred metres, the path narrowed. The wind picked up and I had to stop for a moment.

'I have to pee,' I said, turning to Josh. 'Right now!'

I handed one of my poles to Wyn and turned to the near vertical drop to my right. Josh tensed and held onto my backpack as I tried not to look down at the craggy rocks and swirling fog below.

'I can confirm that it is most definitely minus twelve degrees!' I shouted over the tearing winds.

Bladder emptied, I edged away from the side of the mountain and took my pole from Wyn.

It began to snow. The flakes swirled around us; we could only see five metres in front of us now, but on we went. Right foot forwards, left leg sliding behind.

A cheer of applause drifted through the fog. I had heard the summit before I could see it.

'Come on!' Rich shouted from the top. 'What took you so long?'

'Where the hell have you been?' Lois's brother, Joe, joined in. 'I'm freezing my nads off up here!'

I gave a large grin and the cheers continued as I rounded my way onto the large, rocky outcrop that is the peak of Snowdon. Through the falling snow was the outline of my whittled down group. They were perched amongst the other climbers who had made it to the top. Once they saw me limp around the corner, all of the climbers who I didn't know joined in with the cheering too. The last ten metres were ice-covered steps that had been sheered out of the rock. As I made my way up the twenty steps, right leg leading, I looked around at the strangers, friends and family who had made it to the top with me. My support system had got me here.

I took the final step, bent over and kissed the circular stone trig point that marked the summit.

Looking up, I was met with smiling faces waving bottles of beer and hip flasks at me. Someone had even popped some champagne. I had hardly drank during my training but I wanted to join in with the celebrations. After carefully making my way back down the stone steps, I took a swig from everything that was offered and went around thanking everyone who had made the journey with me. My climb was more special because I had shared it with others.

I had been pretty confident that I would make it to the top but I hadn't been sure of my reaction when I got there. It wasn't until I turned to Lois, the wind whipping her hair across her face, that I realised this wasn't just about climbing a mountain.

Without warning, I was transported back to the intensive care hospital bed, muttering to myself that it would all be okay but not really believing it. I'd been motionless, peering down at my body, willing it to follow the instructions I was sending it to move but getting nothing in return. For a few seconds I was there, as real as stepping back in time; I had thought I'd lost it all.

Lois touched my arm and the pressure snapped me back into the present.

'Congratulations,' she said, reaching up to kiss me on the cheek. 'I knew you would do it.'

'Thank you,' I responded. 'For everything.'

I couldn't have done it without you . . .

The moment was broken by Rich handing me a hip flask, which I swigged from after he shook it in front of my face several times.

'Gah! What was that?' I asked, as I swallowed down the concoction that took part of my oesophagus with it.

'I've been working on a few new blends,' he responded, with the air of a man who had been on a weekend mixology course. 'I call it "Mountain Chaser".'

'More like "Mountain Debaser",' I responded, wondering if the aftertaste would ever leave my mouth.

All too soon, it was time for our descent. Taking my walking poles from Pete, I took one last look at the stairs to the summit and turned for the descent . . . to fall straight onto my face.

No harm was done, but I found it hilarious that my only tumble was when I was standing on top of the mountain. Chuckling to myself, I was dragged to my feet. Mountain Debaser had had its revenge. Settling my features into the serious expression of a mountaineer, I tried again.

'To base camp!' I shouted, brandishing my walking pole high above my head.

By the time we stumbled back into town, everyone I was with was now limping and groaning in pain – and I didn't think it was an expression of their solidarity with me either. It must have seemed that the zombie apocalypse had rolled into Llanberis. Fortunately, the pub didn't board up its windows at our approach.

Seven hours, ten miles, five thousand, nine hundred and thirty-eight kcal, and four hundred and thirty-two pee stops in total.

It was done. I had climbed a mountain.

And now for our reward – our trip to the Philippines. This holiday was our gift to ourselves. Lois and I needed a change of scenery, so when Souto and his girlfriend, Vicki, invited us with them on holiday we jumped at the chance to get away.

Snowdon had made me realise that there are so many benefits to visiting places you are not familiar with and I wanted to share them with others. It's a form of mindfulness where you can take some time away from being bogged down with your own thoughts for a while.

I also knew that you don't have to travel to the other side of the world for this; any stretch of the outdoors will do. A change of scenery works even if it's only a few miles from home – a walk in the countryside can also help stave off low mood. Our ancient ancestors were all nomads; we are meant to wander. By returning to what we are designed to do, it can often help promote feelings of well-being.

After wandering to the other side of the world a week later, I had found myself sitting directly underneath the air conditioning unit in our hotel room. As a man who had comfortably worn a T-shirt at the top of Snowdon, I knew I was going to have problems with overheating in the Philippines.

As I enjoyed the cool air blasting over my head, I couldn't decide whether I'd be able to make it to the boat that was taking us to the island of Bohol without having to change into a spare T-shirt. One of the ongoing effects of my accident was an inability to sweat below my nipple line. My body had lost 70 per cent of its cooling efficiency and everything above this line was determined to make up the difference.

Looking around the hotel room, I realised that I certainly hadn't travelled this far to sit indoors all day. Heat regulation issues would just have to be dealt with; I'd come here to explore. Hoisting my rucksack onto my back, I glanced longingly at the air conditioning unit before departing the room. Our mantra for this holiday was 'Just attack it' and that's what I was going to do.

Sand is not the best surface for someone who can't lift their foot. Gone were my sliders and flip-flop days and instead I had to wear trainers most of the time while on the pale white beaches. I didn't mind. Fashionable footwear was an easy trade for being able to visit a succession of near-deserted island beaches with few tourists and plenty of coconuts to sip from.

Whilst on holiday, I'd carried on with my rehab every day. There were no massive lie-ins or full days spent around the pool. Perhaps it wasn't what most people would call a relaxing break, but I already felt re-energised and ready for what was coming next.

Today, one of the locals had offered to take us out to the edge of the reef. As we approached his boat, all four of us eyed it up. There was no pier and we would have to wade our way out to it. It was pretty small, and this meant that it bobbed up and down with every rolling wave.

'I'm just going to attack,' I said, looking at the frown of concern on Souto's face.

'Perhaps we should ask some of the locals if they can help lift you in?'

'Nope,' I responded. 'Attack.'

This was the thing – boats have steep sides (I am reliably told that it helps keep the water out). And my foot lifted three inches on a good day. I therefore had to figure out how to raise something that lifted only three inches up another three feet. This was particularly a problem if the boat in question had all the stability of a seesaw.

Thankfully, Souto is a pretty big guy and could give me a leg up. With the water up to our thighs, I had no choice but to launch the rest of myself over the side. And that's how I ended up flat on my back in a canoe-sized boat off one of the smaller islands of the Philippines.

Once I managed to right myself, we puttered out to the edge of the reef. With my snorkelling mask firmly in place, I half-rolled, half-fell into the sea. An explosion of colour awaited me under the surface. Brightly coloured fish of every shade swam in shoals around the drifting coral. I swam towards them; the ease of movement in the salted water had put me on a level playing field with the others in our group. I could dive, turn and twist in a way that I would never be granted above the surface.

When I was younger, I would regularly snorkel in the ocean with my younger brother. Often we would swim down fifteen or twenty metres and tap the divers on the shoulder. They would turn, expecting to see their wetsuit clad friend and instead were confronted by a 12-year-old in speedos. I therefore knew that if I wanted to find the more interesting (bigger) fish I would need to locate the reef wall and drop off.

Leading the way, I glided above the ten-foot-deep reef. An inky shadow was up ahead, and I swam towards it. With little announcement, the reef dropped away into blackness. All along the reef wall, facing the darkened well, were the brightest corals rippling in the sea.

I took a deep breath and down I dived. There was a shimmering pink fan coral perched on the edge of the wall and I aimed for that. Feeling good at this depth, I decided to equalise and kicked on past it to stare into the abyss. There's a heady feeling that comes with staring down into the darkness of the sea. It's partly fear of something that is so deep that sunlight can't penetrate it and partly exhilaration that you are on the edge of the unknown.

Deciding to be sensible, I began to surface for air. On the way up, I passed a turtle snoozing amongst the corals. If you have never seen turtles in the wild before, you might not know they are without a doubt the most docile creatures you will come across. He turned his head to study me. I hung there, watching him; it was just the two of us sizing each other up. Not wishing to disturb him, I kicked my way up to the surface and took a lungful of air.

An hour later, after hauling myself back into the boat with all the elegance of an aged walrus, I sat back and gazed out at the sea. I tried to process what had just happened. I had seen all of those sights before, I hadn't gone deeper or longer without air. Far from it. So why did I feel so happy? Why did I feel like I'd just had the experience of a lifetime?

It was because in the water I was free again. Free from all of the problems that I faced on land. Underneath the surface of the sea, no one had to wait for me to catch up, or help me negotiate a particularly tricky section. I was back to being the 12-year-old boy who used to dive too deeply with his brother. The sea had gifted me a short reprise into my past, away from my physical limitations, and I was grateful.

CHAPTER 16

A FIREMAN AND A BALLERINA

Eight years earlier . . .

The party was fancy dress and the theme was 'What do you want to be when you grow up?' At the age of 21, I still felt that this was a valid question, so I went all out.

Straightening my rented fireman's helmet, I rang the front doorbell. As with most student accommodation in Bath, the flat was pretty snug and there were twelve of us crammed into the living room. One of my rugby friends was dating a university student and it was her birthday that we were celebrating on that cold January evening.

Sitting on the floor, surrounded by friends in various costumes, I thought that there was no better way to chivvy along the early January weeks. The doorbell rang again, and I turned to see who would be joining us. We already had a pirate, doctor, snow boarder and a guy who was ironically dressed as himself. In entered a tall blonde in a tutu, leotard and pink tights. Her smile lit up when she realised the party was already in full swing and I watched as she greeted the birthday girl. She had an air of openness that I liked and seemed completely at ease in her surroundings.

As the room heated up, I ditched the helmet and jacket as my outfit was entirely polyester and I was starting to boil inside of it. I patted down my newly zipped hair, pleased that I'd managed to cut out all of the bleached blond spikes. It had been turning a light shade of green from the chlorine in the pool I swam in every week and there had finally been an intervention by Rich and Tom. Apparently, I had looked like a chorus puppet from *Sesame Street*.

An hour later, the ballerina plonked herself down next to me.

'Bloody hell,' she said, 'my tutu got trapped in the oven when Clare put the pizzas on. I think I'm better sitting down for a bit.'

I smiled at her and shifted over to make way for the sprays of netting.

'I'm Ed,' I said, putting my can of Stella down to shake her hand in a mock formal way.

'And I'm Lois,' she said, grasping my hand.

Six hours later we were drunkenly singing 'Purple Rain' by Prince at each other in the Second Bridge nightclub in Bath. We had already cleared the dance floor and together we pirouetted off to get our coats.

Outside, I plucked up the courage to ask her something that I never asked other girls. I faffed around with the collar of my coat until I forced myself to meet her eye.

'Can I have your number?' I asked, the cold stinging my cheeks.

'Ed,' Lois said, staring straight at me, 'this will be the third time you've asked me that, and the third time I've given it to you.'

'Oh,' I responded, checking my phone. Sure enough, there it was. 'I must have drunk a bit too much tonight. Can I buy you a kebab then?'

Lois linked her arm through mine. 'Of course you can. Mine's a doner, please. And don't spare the garlic mayo.'

Eight years later, I was standing under an air-conditioning unit in only my pants and Souto was advancing towards me with a pair of scissors.

'It's just that tufty bit at the back,' he said. 'It's got to go.'

It was thirty-five degrees outside and I really didn't want to leave my prime spot under the cooling air. Equally, I didn't want Souto to cut my hair.

'I'm sure it's fine,' I said to Souto, while keeping my back firmly up against the wall.

'Right,' Rich said, checking his watch. 'We have twenty minutes to go until it's game on. So you have to get into your suit.'

I glanced over at the linen jacket and trousers that were hanging on the outside of the wardrobe, freshly pressed by my mum that morning. The air outside was so still that it felt like forty degrees. I knew I'd sweat through my suit within half an hour, so I was trying to leave it off for as long as possible. Lois would look stunning in whatever she wore and I didn't want to let the team down.

Rich was right, it was time for the suit. Excitement bubbled up in me as I pulled on the dark trousers and light-coloured jacket I'd bought especially for this occasion. I was going to get married . . . I was going to marry the girl that I loved.

The sound of scissors snapping together made me turn around.

'Got it,' Souto said, holding up a rather large lock of hair. 'Much better now.'

I looked at Rich who shrugged.

It was game time.

Twenty minutes later, holding onto Rich, I made my way down the four stone steps from the villa. With him walking close by my side, I carried on along the uneven white gravel until I reached the garden where the ceremony would take place. Rich slowed and moved behind me, and I walked down the aisle by myself without the use of a crutch or walking pole. This is what had spurred me on all those months ago – I didn't want to use a wheelchair or stick when I walked down the aisle to get married. I took it slowly and grinned at everyone who turned to face me from their white cane chairs.

The scent of lavender and rosemary filled the air. We were in the rustic gardens of the villa and behind the officiant was an ancient olive tree that had been decorated with glass beads. It was the perfect setting.

Standing at the end of the aisle, I listened to the saxophonist as he played through the gentle melodies that would accompany the service. Rich, as my best man, stood by my side holding a folded hanky for me to wipe the perspiration from my face. There wasn't a puff of air to break the intense heat and the low buzzing of the cicadas only served to intensify the stillness surrounding us.

The saxophonist slipped seamlessly into 'L-O-V-E' by Nat King Cole and I looked up to see Lois approaching on her father's arm. She was radiant, wearing a tight-fitting silk dress that suited her to perfection. The cream hues complemented her summer tan as the long veil trailed behind her. My heart swelled with pride that this woman would be my wife. As she broke away from her father's arm, she stepped towards me and we kissed. Everyone cheered and we grinned at each other. The kiss was supposed to be at the end of the ceremony, but we didn't care.

As we turned towards the registrar, the months of pain and uncertainty were all worth it, just to be here with her. I blinked away the tears and tried to focus on the words of the officiant. We started by sealing the letters we had written to each other to be opened on our ten-year wedding anniversary. As the ribbon was tied around them, I was overcome by a feeling of light-headedness. I put my arm out to steady myself. The heat was too much for me.

The officiant frowned and whispered, 'Are you all right? Shall I move it along a bit?'

'Yes, please,' I whispered back.

She whizzed through the next section and then we were repeating our vows.

'Up until this moment,' the officiant said, 'you have been many things to each other. Acquaintance, friend, companion, lover and teacher. For you have learnt much from each other over these past years. You are now about to say a few words that will take you across a threshold in life. For after these vows, you shall say to the world, "This is my husband", and, "This is my wife." Can we have the rings, please, Rich?'

Rich brought them over to us, his smile so wide that his eyes creased at the corners.

I slipped the ring onto the end of Lois's finger. 'I give you this ring as a symbol of my love and faithfulness. As I place it on your finger, I commit my heart and soul to you. I ask you to wear this ring as a reminder of the vows we have spoken today, our wedding day.'

I pushed the ring further onto her finger, but it was stuck.

Lois laughed and tried to push it on.

'It's a bit warm,' I said.

'It's a bit swollen,' she responded, finally managing to get it on.

The guests laughed and we relaxed into the moment.

Lois placed a gold band onto the end of my finger. 'I give you this ring to wear with love and joy. As a ring has no end, neither shall my love for you. I choose you to be my husband for this day and evermore.'

'Ed, you may kiss your bride.'

And I did.

The cheers of our wedding guests drowned out the hum of the cicadas. I couldn't stop watching Lois as she smiled at everyone. She had already proven that she would be by my side, for better or for worse.

I took her hand and we walked back down the aisle together, as husband and wife.

Our honeymoon was a more relaxed affair than we had anticipated. We spent our time sleeping, eating and exploring the countryside of Tuscany. We were both tired from the build-up to the wedding and needed to allow ourselves to do very little.

When we arrived in Rome, on the last leg of the honeymoon, we were both beginning to feel like ourselves again. We had a friend who was from Rome and had given us a list of all the small restaurants that the Italians liked to keep to themselves, away from the tourist trail. We managed to get a table at one of them, squished into the corner, and we enjoyed hearing the chatter of the locals as we tried to guess what they were saying.

I peered at the menu in the soft candlelight as I pondered my selection. I felt relaxed, happy . . . at peace. We had needed this time together to reconnect and plan what was coming next. Lois had started gently asking me about what I hoped to do in the coming months. I'd been pondering this for most of our honeymoon.

'I think I've made a decision,' I said, looking up at Lois.

'Oh, yes? What are you going to have?'

'Not from the menu, I can't decide between four of the dishes.' I shuffled closer on my small chair. 'I meant what I'm going to do over the next few months.'

Lois leant forwards.

'I'm going to train to climb Mont Buet in France. And then I'm going to climb it.'

'Mont Buet! But that's, what?' Lois wrinkled her brow. 'Twice as high as Snowdon?'

'Three times actually,' I responded, grinning at her. 'I think it will take two days to do.'

'Two days!'

I let Lois ponder it for a moment. I'd just sprung this news on her and she needed a moment to adjust.

'It's safe, isn't it?'

'Of course it is.'

I had already decided not to mention the avalanche that had killed a skier a couple of years before. There was no need to worry her.

'It's just whether I'll make it to the top. That's the question. There's the altitude to contend with, which we didn't have at Snowdon, for a start.

'Well, if you want to do it, I'll fully support you,' Lois said, taking a sip from her wine glass.

'I want to climb it with lots of other people. Just like Snowdon. Only longer, higher and slightly more dangerous.'

'Well,' she said, 'we'd better start planning this.'

A week after I got home from Italy, I received an important email. It was from Nas, my fellow patient at Salisbury Spinal Unit. He wanted to let me know that he had carried on with his rehab after I had been discharged and he was now able to walk with crutches.

I leant back in the wheelchair that I used to sit at my desk – a daily reminder of what I could still be using – and thought of Nas walking around his newly modified flat. He hadn't needed most of the modifications in the end as he'd decided to hope for something, even if it might not come to him.

Back when I was in hospital, many people had said, 'We don't want to give you false hope.' I was against this notion. What was wrong with false hope? Without it you were just left with 'no hope'. I thought of all the people across the country who might have been held back with their recovery because of lack of hope or information.

Hope had also provided me with other opportunities while I was striving for my original goal, because I had been open to new possibilities. Before my accident, I had thought a lot about what I would do after my rugby career ended in a few years' time. I'd known that I would have to make a change and prepare for the future. So, in my mid-twenties, I had started studying for a degree and was halfway through a Masters in Real Estate Finance when my accident happened. I'd decided that when I grew up for the second time in my life, I was going to work in commercial property.

Recently, I had been offered a couple of days a week working as an intern at a big firm in London, so I set off to the City. This was an area of work that a lot of ex-rugby players moved to when their careers had ended. Before my accident happened, I knew it would suit me perfectly. I would play golf at the weekends and possibly move back to Clapham, where I had lived early in my rugby career. I liked golf and I liked Clapham. So, why, at the end of my internship, didn't I feel as enthused about it as I had been a few years ago?

It was because the accident had changed me in more ways than one. It had altered my hopes for the future and my values as well. Once I was introduced to the joys of helping others and raising money for charity, I couldn't let go of the idea that this was what I was meant to do. I allowed myself to hope that I would do this for the rest of my life. And somehow earn enough to provide food and shelter for me and Lois.

Having been paid to speak at some conferences and business events, I had started to earn a bit of money. I did these alongside a lot of free charity and hospital talks. However, I hadn't been prepared for one of the biggest surprises that was a consequence of my accident.

A month after my wedding, I had a call from a production company who had apparently been silently stalking me at my talks. Unknown to me, they had attended a few and thought I would do well on television. Then came the news that made my head spin – Channel 4 had asked me to work as a reporter for the rugby season that was starting in November.

I had been offered a job I wouldn't have even thought about chasing. All because I took a different path from the one that was expected of me.

I was going to be on TV!

CHAPTER 17

ICE BREAKER

Almost eighteen months after my accident, there were nineteen of us sitting around a large table in an oak-panelled chalet in France. It was the evening before we began climbing Mont Buet, and most of us had only met for the first time a few hours ago. I was feeling the pressure to make this a success, as it was the first time I had attended a climb that was abroad. At three times the height of Snowdon, and with the altitude to consider, it was going to take two days to climb. I had no idea if my body was going to hold out for that long, but I was looking forward to testing myself.

As I tucked into my starter, I realised that several of my co-hikers were staring intently into their soup bowls and saying very little. They had decided to raise money for Restart, the rugby charity that supports all premiership players in England and which had paid for my physio, by climbing a mountain with a bunch of strangers.

I nudged my stepmum, Sue, who was sitting next to me. 'Some of them haven't said anything.'

At that moment one of the organisers of the trip stood up and suggested that we all go around and introduce ourselves and explain why we were there.

'Good idea,' Sue said. 'I'll start the ball rolling.'

Sue pushed her chair back and stood up.

'I'm Ed's stepmum, Sue. Ed's dad and I have been together for thirteen years and I have a son who plays rugby as well. So, we've had a rugby family together for many years. But it wasn't until seventeen months ago, when the biggest upset happened, that I became aware of Restart's work. I was in the pool on the day . . . which was obviously very . . .'

Sue stopped for a moment to gather herself and we all called out our encouragement for her to continue.

'Sorry. It was very difficult. As I'm sure you can all imagine. Supporting Ed, his dad, his family and our melded family was my number one priority. I've seen what an amazing job Restart has done. I climbed Snowdon last year with Ed.' Sue beamed around the table. 'And when Ed asked me to come on this trip, I was so happy. It meant so much that he would want to include me.'

I leant over and squeezed her arm and she smiled down at me.

'It's always difficult combining families,' Sue continued, 'but I hope you soon find out that I love Ed just as much as my own children. I am so thrilled with the improvement he's made and all the help he has had. And that's partly down to Restart, so I wanted to help him raise money for them.'

After Sue's brilliant start, there was hardly a dry eye in the place. One by one, we gave our own reasons for being there. There were ex-rugby players who wanted to return some of the help they had received, supporters of the rugby players' union and a couple of people who wished to try climbing a mountain for the first time. Everyone gave their reasons and they were all good ones.

The ice had begun to break, but all too soon we had to disperse and get some sleep, in preparation for the big day.

The emotional charge of that evening was still with me in the morning. Although I hadn't said it to anyone, I was hoping that I hadn't taken on too much. I'd never walked for two consecutive days before, or up such a steep incline, and I'd never had to contend with altitude sickness. I knew that the first day would be easier, but would I be too tired to tackle the twelve-hour second day? There were so many variables that I'd tried to prepare for, but I couldn't cover everything. As always, fear of the unknown was testing me. I had to put into practice what I'd always told myself – that the feeling of fear was always worse than the experience itself. I'd proven this to myself countless times.

As we emerged from our chalet in Buet village and got into the cars that would take us to the start of our climb, we were met by a bright September sun that threatened a temperature in the mid-twenties by lunchtime. This may sound like the perfect climate, but it really wasn't for this amount of physical exertion, especially for someone who couldn't sweat properly. We would be staying overnight on the way up the mountain, so the bag I was carrying that morning was much heavier than I was used to. We had four kilometres to walk before lunch, which included 250 vertical metres.

One of our guides for the next few days was a French man named Seb who quickly led us onto the first track. Within a few hundred metres, the steep angle we were walking at meant that every step required extra energy. We all fell silent as the reality of what our bodies were required to do over the next few days became clear. The winding path narrowed, and I slowly dropped to the back as I struggled with the uneven terrain. I tried not to get frustrated by being last and reminded myself how lucky I was to even be there. To my left was the open vista with its breathtaking views of the mountain range, and to my right was the rugged greenery and trees that clung to the mountain side.

Seb stuck with me the entire way, helping me decide where to place my feet when needed. Our group began to stretch out as the fitter ones pushed ahead with another one of the guides.

The morning passed relatively quickly, and we stopped for a lunch of doughy bread stuffed with slabs of ham and cheese. When climbing these types of terrain, my body will burn around seven thousand calories a day, whereas other people will burn between three and five thousand. I burn more calories than most people because I walk a bit like Quasimodo. It means that with every step I use more energy, closer to what another person would use if they were jogging. So plentiful meals were essential. We all ate well before setting off to cover the next seven kilometres that would take us a further 375 metres above sea level.

Our pace was steady, and by 3 p.m. we reached the dormitory we would be sharing for the night. Judging by the looks of mild horror on some of my co-hikers' faces, they hadn't been prepared for the realities of sharing one dorm and one toilet with twenty other people. For my part, I didn't mind too much about our accommodation standards as I hadn't had much privacy on the hospital wards. However, I was annoyed that I had to bow out of the optional hike to a lake that was to the east of our lodge. My legs were burning and my knee had begun to swell so I had to be sensible. A couple of years ago, I would have been the first out of the door to visit a mountain lake that I could bathe in. But then, I reminded myself, eighteen months ago no one thought I would walk again – you win some, and you lose some.

For the rest of the afternoon I sat outside our communal lodging. The mental focus required for hiking was an act of mindfulness for me and, although shattered, I felt at peace whenever I finished a day in the mountains.

Despite this, I had begun to find it difficult to ignore the stares I was receiving from some of the French people who were also sharing our accommodation. All day, as we passed people descending the mountain and were overtaken by others ascending it, I had received an unusual amount of attention. The other hikers would look at my heavily strapped, slightly twisted leg and almost wince. I had noticed that Seb had stopped to talk to the other hikers when we had our regular breaks, but I couldn't understand the rapidly fired French passing between them. Seb was a legend on these mountains. As one of the regular guides, it seemed as if he knew everyone and I had presumed that he was catching up with his associates and friends.

Seb and the others returned from the lake just as the sun began to set outside our cabin. The first thing Seb did was make a beeline to check on me. I explained that my knee was aching less and that I would try to walk to the lake if I ever came back again. He sat down next to me and we watched the orange flares of the sunset sink below the horizon. After a few minutes of comfortable silence, I decided to ask him a question.

'I know I'm not your "average" hiker but I've never received this many awkward looks. Do you know why?'

'Ah, that,' he said, in excellent English. 'Some French people have strong opinions about these things. They do not understand why a man who struggles to walk would want to climb a mountain. Some think the notion is ridiculous and that you should keep yourself safe and away from further things that could injure you.'

'Oh,' I responded.

Well, I had asked him a question. I should have prepared myself for an answer that perhaps I didn't want to hear.

'What were you saying to them on the climb up, then?'

'I was telling everyone your story. I wanted them to know that you had a reason for being here. And that it was a good one.'

I smiled to myself.

'Thanks, Seb,' I responded, while gazing at the last rays of the sunset.

We did not sleep well. But then, the odds were against us. In a dormitory of twenty people, there were bound to be several snorers who would keep everyone awake. After a couple of hours of tossing and turning, I slipped into a fitful sleep and probably added to the cacophony surrounding me.

The evening before, Seb had told us we would split into two groups to make the final climb. I had been assigned to the slower of the two groups that would be setting off at 5 a.m. The fitter, more experienced group, would be leaving an hour behind us at six.

Leaving the warm shelter, the first group stumbled into the darkness of the early morning. Each of us had a torch strapped to our head and the light shining out from it only picked out the few metres in front. Sue walked with me, our beams bobbing next to one another. As the path narrowed, we dropped into a single line, snaking our way up the first of the trails.

As we climbed higher, the greenery around us died out and we were faced with the gravelled mountain side. We spread out and Seb began guiding my every step. The terrain we were now climbing was so steep it was close to vertical at some points. Everyone in our group had to use walking poles to help them navigate their way. The gravel-like texture of the mountain side meant my foot would often slip from beneath me. The closer we got to the summit, the more I relied on Seb to guide and support me. And this was all done with just our torch beams for light.

I didn't want to hold anyone up, and I certainly didn't want the other group catching up with us straight away, so I only stopped when the first tentative rays of light began to emerge over the mountain range. All around us were the white tipped peaks of the Alps. Once again, I was reminded of how I never thought I would see these sights again.

'The boulder field is next,' Seb said, standing next to me. 'We had better continue.'

I nodded in agreement; the view would still be here in a few hours' time.

I had read about the boulder field but nothing could have prepared me for it when a twist in the mountain path revealed its looming presence.

'Oh, shit,' I said, stopping for a moment. 'How am I going to get up that?'

'With my help,' Seb responded.

Imagine a chunky gravel driveway. Then tip it up to an angle so acute that you can't believe all the gravel isn't sliding down to the bottom. Finally, shrink yourself down to the size of a Borrower and try to climb up it. This was what I was facing. To cross the boulder field, you had to step and hop from one boulder to the next and some of the boulders were the size of small cars. One misplaced footing would send your leg plummeting down the gap between them, resulting in a nasty sprain or worse.

Seb helped pull me up onto the first boulder. While I tried to keep my balance, he surveyed our options.

'That one over there,' he said, pointing to a boulder to our right.

Holding onto his arm, I stepped towards the boulder. Using my walking poles to engage the strength from my top half, I pulled my reluctant left leg onto the second boulder and took a moment.

'Maybe that one there,' I said, pointing to a boulder directly in front.

'No, I think not,' Seb said. 'It looks as if it could rock under your weight. That one there is a safer option.'

I was putting all my faith into Seb, a man I had only met two days ago.

With the next step, I had to lead with my left leg and was able to push my stronger right leg across to meet it.

On we went, up this sheer mountain of ancient rock. Seb stuck by my side at every step while also keeping a watchful eye over the rest of our group. I can honestly say I wouldn't have been able to do it without him.

When I clambered down from the final boulder, panting from the exertion, we all agreed to stop for half an hour to eat an early lunch. The 6 a.m. group caught up with us shortly afterwards and we were pleased to be summiting together. Packing up, we pushed on, with Seb still by my side, helping me with every step.

When I occasionally glanced up from staring at my feet, I noticed that the French people who were coming down the mountainside were now tipping their hats at me. They were also saying '*chapeau*', which means 'hats off to you', as they passed our group. Instead of looks of confusion, I was now receiving looks of admiration. Seb's supportive words had obviously spread both up and down the mountainside.

Two hours later, after zoning out and concentrating on just putting one foot in front of the other, everyone dropped behind me as we made our way up the final kilometre of the stark grey peak of the mountain. There was no snow or ice to contend with as there had been at Snowdon, but I could honestly say that the climb was the hardest physical challenge I had encountered. Its steepness and duration tested me all the way.

The summit was covered in loose rocks and I had to concentrate on every step as my trusty walking poles helped with the final few steps. Three thousand feet above sea level and only three more strides to go.

And then, to cheers all around me, I reached the top. I had done it.

Looking around over the sprawling alpine range towards Mont Blanc, Seb pointed out the five countries that could be seen from my vantage point. My love for the mountains had solidified and I knew it would remain within me for the rest of my life. To my embarrassment, tears began to form. It was overwhelming to know how far the support of my friends and family had brought me less than a year and a half after my accident. I was so grateful to be alive. I was so grateful to be able to walk again. I knew that I was one of the lucky ones.

Everyone crowded around me as we congratulated each other. Try as I might, I couldn't stop my tears. My cheeks flushed as everyone turned to me, expecting me to say a few words.

I cleared my throat and raised my head to address the eighteen people who had made this journey with me. I had to smile. I had gone from being a tough rugby player who never showed any sort of emotion, to someone who wept at the beauty of being alive at the top of the Alps – and I was okay with that.

'Sorry,' I said, wiping the tears away. 'I just remembered that we have to walk back down again.'

Even though I was laughing along with everyone else, the tears still kept on coming.

'It's going to be short speech as I'm a bit emotional,' I said, while wiping my face again. 'For a long time, I didn't think that I'd visit places like this again. And that's why we should never take things like this for granted, because a lot of people can't do this. Focus on the things in your life that are positive, the things that you already have, not the things that you don't. It's been an amazing, positive experience for me and I hope it has been for you.'

Everyone cheered and we grinned at each other.

Now we just had to get down the mountain.

It turned out that getting down was just as hard as getting up. And not just for me. Everyone had to concentrate on their footing as the loose stones meant that in a split second your legs could go from underneath you. This was difficult enough on the way up, but throw gravity into the equation and you could easily see yourself sliding down the mountainside, gathering pace all the way.

But down we went.

Strangely, the way back down was just as motivating for me as the way up and this was solely because of two people I had the pleasure of walking with. Damien and Ally were the owners of the tour company that had facilitated the climb. I hadn't spent much time with them before, but, on the way back down, they took to helping me with the perilous descent with gusto. Across the boulder fields we went, past the place we stayed for the night, until we reached the steep trails that led us back to Buet village.

As they guided me through the many pitfalls, their story naturally came out. Both of them had enjoyed successful corporate careers but had always longed for something else. Their greatest pleasure came from the mountains. When Damien was offered what should have been a dream corporate job, he turned it down after Ally persuaded him that it was the right thing to do. He wanted to realise his actual dreams, not what everyone expected of him. So, he and Ally turned their backs on that life and set up a company that combined performance coaching with guided tours of their favourite mountain ranges. And they had made a success of it. They also organised fundraising trips for charities, so Damien and Ally's values had finally aligned with their work.

All the way down the mountainside, I noticed how everyone in our group was laughing and chatting with each other, helping each other along the way. The mountain had broken any ice that had lingered between this group of mostly strangers and there was a natural camaraderie that normally only comes after years of friendship.

Speaking to Ally and Damien broadened my horizons of what was possible. It gave me the confidence to start considering whether Lois and I could set up a charity together. The cogs in my head had begun to turn and I couldn't wait to get back home and speak to Lois about it.

When we finally reached Buet village, we were all limping after twelve hours on our aching feet. There is a special sort of bond that grows between people when they participate in something this intense. The walk had equalised us, united us. As everyone hobbled to the minibuses that would take us to our beds that night, I felt as if I was amongst my closest friends.

I was crossing the field next to our house when I had a thought – did I really need these walking poles? Looking down at my hands, I decided to drop them. They landed with a clatter even though the grass was soft. I took a few steps, kept my balance and something magical happened. With every stride, my left leg straightened and began to take its fair share of my weight. My ankle clicked into place and my foot arch began to strengthen and rise.

Holding my clawed left hand out in front of me, I watched as it unfurled like a budding flower. I hadn't yet realised that I was dreaming. I looked around – I needed someone else to see this and confirm that it was real, but I was alone. I had to get back to the house and tell Lois what had happened.

Quickening my pace, with each step I felt my body respond to these new demands. I broke into a jog. Slowly at first, just to test myself. But the uneven, rough grass was no match for me. With each stride my body reacted instantaneously, subtly tilting me in the direction I needed to keep my balance. The wind picked up and blew behind me, pushing me forwards. I began to sprint, faster and faster . . . I was free.

I blinked open my eyes and for a moment I was still in the field, strength coursing through my body. I had this dream all the time. In the year and a half since my accident, my mind had adjusted and I limped in all my dreams. But then, in some of them, I would make a miraculous recovery in a matter of moments. I would be back to where I started, able to pick up my old life. If I wanted to.

I sat up in bed, hoping to shake the disappointment away. I would never run again, I knew that. That didn't make me miss it any less. Pulling my legs from the bed, I tensed my core as I tried to stand. A spasm hit my left leg and I sat on the edge of the bed again. I stared down at my thighs, my left about a third smaller than my right as the muscle had withered away and never recovered. It was going to be one of those mornings where I couldn't make the few steps to the bathroom without stretching my limbs first.

Glancing down, I checked the catheter bag that I wore every night. Almost full. I'd have to get to the bathroom soon.

I began a series of squats at the end of the bed to try to wake my legs up. My left leg would often lock in the morning and it would take ten to fifteen minutes of repeating these exercises to get it moving again.

When my legs felt more supple, I hobbled along the edge of the bed until I reached the chest of drawers. Holding on to its side, I swung my left leg in a circle to move it forwards, until I reached the chair next to the bathroom door. From there, I took a step and reached out for the door frame. I had to trace my way around the furniture that edged the room so I would have something to hold on to and not fall. There were no direct routes for me in the mornings.

Taking off my catheter, I emptied the bag in the toilet and cleaned all of the equipment. I took a shower, the soap slipping from my clawed left hand. Before putting on my clothes, I attached the orthotics to my leg that would lift my left foot and allow me to step forwards rather than swinging my leg around in a semi-circle. Holding on to the bannister, I took each step at a time as I negotiated the staircase. The dogs needed their morning walks and they circled around my legs, eager to get out for an hour.

Without thinking about it, I walked to the field I had dreamt about. I had my walking poles with me to help steady myself on the uneven terrain. The dogs were off their leads and Molly was bounding farther ahead, while Baz celebrated being out in the crisp winter sun by rolling in the grass.

I looked down at the poles in my hands. What would happen if I threw them to the ground and tried to run? One step and I'd topple over, probably flat on my face. There was no point even thinking about it. I picked up my pace as I'd lost sight of the dogs when they had crested the hill.

'Baz! Molly!'

Their excited barks signalled their position and I aimed for it.

Turning too sharply, my left foot caught the back of my right and I was falling. I dropped my poles, twisted to the side to protect my neck and braced myself.

The impact hit my shoulder first, then my hip, but my neck was safe. I lay there for a moment allowing my breathing to calm and my racing pulse to quieten. Adrenaline coursed around my body, ready to help me if I needed it.

It's okay . . . you're okay. This is just a part of your life now.

Pulling myself up so I was sitting, I called for the dogs. While I waited, I tried to brush some of the mud from my jeans. The dogs raced back to me and Molly circled me protectively. Sometimes, it was as if they knew there was something wrong. Baz padded over and licked my face, which made me grin – now I was covered in mud and dog slobber.

I pulled myself onto my front and pushed up with my stronger right leg and arm. Grabbing my poles, I hobbled back to the house. Perhaps I'd hit my left hip harder than I'd thought. The cold November air was biting at my hands and as I pulled out the key from my pocket, my right hand seized up. My left hand is always curled around – I call it 'The Claw' – so it acts pretty much like a fist. I therefore rely solely on my right hand for anything that requires more finesse than 'Hulk smash'. If my right hand seizes up in cold weather, I'm pretty much screwed.

I tried to fish the key out of my trouser pocket and managed to slide it into my palm, but I'd lost all dexterity in my fingers and couldn't pick it up. That's how I ended up spending the next half an hour with my hands clamped between my thighs, trying to warm them up so I could get indoors.

With less time available than I had anticipated, I began to pack up what I needed to attend a talk that evening. Into my bag went a spare catheter, change of clothes and pants in case of an accident. I'd only be away for a few hours but a lot can happen in that amount of time. About six months before, I'd had an 'accident' on the A4174 that required me to drive all the way home to shower and change – it wasn't a wee accident either. Fortunately, my bowels were now a bit more under control, but my unruly bladder still meant I either had to wear a catheter or stay within fifty metres of a toilet. Those were my choices.

I switched my orthotics for the electrical FES, packed up all the spare batteries and pads for it and waited for Lois to get home from work so she could do up the cuffs of my shirt. Surveying my large backpack, I thought about how I used to take less on a weekend away. All chances of spontaneity had gone.

Shirt sleeves done, I got into my automatic car, checked my catheter again and drove the ninety-minute journey. I wanted to arrive early so I could scope out where the toilets were.

As I walked down the carpeted entranceway of the plush building, I recognised an old acquaintance I hadn't seen for a few months.

'Ed,' he said, stepping forwards and shaking my hand enthusiastically, 'you look fantastic. And I heard about your climbs up Snowdon and Buet. You must almost be back to normal now.'

I suppose none of us ever really knows what lies beneath.

CHAPTER 18

PATHWAYS

When my younger brother and I were children, we developed an all-encompassing addiction to video games. Hours were spent kneeling nose-close to the TV screen. PlayStation controllers were launched at each other's heads if there was any perceived cheating or unfair advantage. One time, we argued for so long over Donkey Kong in the backseat of our parents' car that my dad ordered us to throw our Game Boys out of the window. After pleading with him for half the length of the M4, he wouldn't relent. So, with many tears and plans to call grandparents to inform them of the depths of our mistreatment, two much loved games consoles were thrown out of the window of our Mitsubishi Shogun.

When we got home, all of our consoles, games and comic books were taken away and in return we were both given a subscription to the *National Geographic*. Our mum believed this would encourage us to read and broaden our horizons beyond memorising maps for Golden Eye or the tracks of Mario Cart. We believed it was one step down from child abuse.

But, much to everyone's surprise, it worked. Before long, we were both hooked and back outside again building dens in the garden.

One edition of the magazine in particular has always remained with me – Nepal. So, to be stepping off a plane in one of the countries I'd fantasised about since I was a boy was pretty special.

It was a month after I had climbed Mont Buet and this time it was just me and Lois journeying together. After two days of travel, three flights and five thousand miles, we arrived in Chitwan, which was to be our home for the next few days. We had been invited over by Neverest Orthopaedics, a charity that was trying to raise money for a new spinal unit in Nepal. I had heard about them through a family friend who was an orthopaedic surgeon and I'd agreed to go over and visit to help raise awareness. Helping them gave me some purpose. Lois and I hadn't done anything like this before and weren't sure what to expect.

As we made our way through the small corrugated iron shed that served as an airport, Lois nudged me. 'I think they're here for you.'

Following her gaze, I saw a group of people who were beaming at everyone who passed. At the front were our family friends, Geraint and Carole, who had told us about Neverest Orthopaedics and had helped organise the trip for us.

Stumbling under the weight of my bags, I was already profusely sweating as we approached the small crowd and introduced ourselves. In a flash, we were relieved of our luggage and a flurry of handshakes and namastes ensued.

'I'm so glad you've finally made it out here,' Carole said, as she led me to the cars that were to take us on a tour of Chitwan.

'Who are all these people?' I asked, trying to keep my voice down.

'Some of the spinal surgeons and doctors who work at the unit, a few local dignitaries and some supporters of the project.'

I glanced around at Lois who was happily chatting away to our welcoming party. We hadn't had a reception like this since our wedding.

'Who do they think we are?' I whispered to Carole.

'There's not much interest in the spinal unit over here. Anyone who they think can help always gets a grand welcome.'

'Well, let's get started,' I said, as I pulled open the car door.

The first stop was the proposed site for the new spinal unit. Chitwan itself is in the lowlands of Nepal, which is the farthest area from the Himalayas in the north. It has a large national park that borders India and most of the landscape is made of jungle.

Our car turned off the main road and, as we bounced along the dirt track, I couldn't help but peer up at the surrounding canopy. Vines and creepers circled their way around the tree trunks, linking the foliage together for the monkeys to climb across. Thick bushes covered the ground, impassable outside of the trails, and hiding the animals of the jungle. I felt as though as I was being driven towards the gates of Jurassic Park.

When the cars pulled up, I got out of ours as quickly as I could – I was eager to hear about their vision for the spinal unit. Fourteen of us stood in the clearing where the trees had already been felled. Wood chips were scattered on the ground, which gave me an idea of the size of the hospital. Up above, the calls of unfamiliar birds and animals balanced our own chatter below.

'It will be an eighteen-bed hospital,' the translator informed us.

'How much will that cost to build?' I asked, trying to tot up possible numbers in my head.

'We think it will be £250,000.'

I couldn't believe it. With that sort of money, you could build a house in the UK but never something that could transform the lives of eighteen people and their families.

As we talked, I was taken down to the river that acted as a natural border to the national park. Although the site was only fifty metres from the main road, it felt like I was miles away from the bustling streets that had led us here. Staring up at the dappled light that filtered its way through the lush green leaves above, I thought back to my time in Horatio's Garden at Salisbury Spinal Unit and how that outside space had aided my recovery. I was therefore pleased to hear that architects for the spinal unit in Chitwan planned on leaving as much of the natural habitat intact as they could while creating an outside space for the patients. After you've been lying on a bed inside for weeks or even months, feeling the sun on your face or breathing fresh air can be such a positive, life-affirming experience.

We explored every part of the site and then went for a meal at a nearby hotel where stories were exchanged and tentative plans were drawn. Before I knew it, jet lag had set in. Lois and I made our way to our hotel room and the most inviting-looking bed I had seen for a long time. I closed my eyes with a vision of what I thought the new spinal unit could be. And what an exciting vision it was.

One of my favourite things about this part of the world is that it's socially acceptable to eat curry for breakfast. Chuck a few eggs on top and I was set for the day.

We had been invited to meet the local mayor. This confirmed our suspicions that everyone had mistaken us to be far more important than we actually were. That morning, Lois and I had put on the best clothes our backpacks could provide and I had even ironed my T-shirt. When we arrived at the council buildings, we were whisked from the waiting room into the mayor's office. Giant Nepali flags and pictures of the Himalayas adorned the walls, leaving us in no doubt that we were in the right place.

From behind a large desk emerged Mayor Dahal, a petite woman who was not much older than me but who had the presence of a lioness. Fortunately, a few of the spinal unit doctors had come along to introduce us and help translate. We were invited to sit and I began to explain how excited I was about the project and what I hoped would come from it. Mayor Dahal listened patiently and when she spoke it was with a wisdom that surpassed her years. It soon became very clear why she was in her post.

As the mayor listened intently, she nodded and smiled at me graciously. I'm not entirely sure if the doctor who was acting as my interpreter was deliberately adjusting the translation of my drivel in a way to please the mayor, but the amount of nodding and smiling I was receiving was reassuring.

The reason I had been invited to speak with the mayor was to thank her for donating the land for the spinal unit. Funding for any type of rehabilitation in Nepal is almost non-existent as the limited funds are funnelled into maternity services. And rightfully so. The infant mortality rate is as high as 50 per cent in some regions of Nepal. Rehabilitation always falls behind acute care in all countries; we are just lucky that in the UK we have the NHS to provide a basic level. Without a well-funded national health system, next to nothing filters through to rehab and this results in an area that is in desperate need of support. With that in mind, we were incredibly grateful that Mayor Dahal had arranged for the land to be donated.

All too soon our hour was up. With a final namaste, Lois and I left the room. I was all fired up; it really felt like we could make a difference.

At the entrance to Chitwan's current spinal unit, I was met by a big lad in a wheelchair. Through the translator we introduced ourselves and I found out that he was a former patient who regularly visited the hospital to provide support and counselling. We got chatting and he told me that he had been left paraplegic after a serious traffic accident.

'How did you injure your spine?' he asked.

'Well . . . ah . . . I dived into the shallow end of a swimming pool. I thought it was deeper than it was. There was a really pretty waterfall that made the surface of the pool gently ripple . . .'

As I kept on talking, I could feel my man points were reducing in his head. It wasn't the first time that I'd wished that if I had to suffer a spinal injury then at least I could have done it in some daring escape, possibly involving a motorbike chase and an extended free-fall parachute jump. But I suppose we all have to work with what we've got.

The fact that there appeared to be regular accidents over there that would rarely happen in the UK had not been lost on me. The Nepali people had more natural disasters to contend with than we did back home. The sad truth was that most people died from their injuries, especially up in the mountains, as they wouldn't be able to get to hospital in time to have the lifesaving surgery they needed.

Taking in the dilapidated frontage of the spinal injury hospital, I noticed how most of the windows were caged or covered. It looked more like a prison than a place of rehabilitation.

We went into the building and stopped in a small room made entirely from bare concrete with a single rusty fan slowly turning in the corner.

I ducked my head to enter the room and was met with a huge grin from a young man lying on the wrought-iron bed. Pressing my palms together, I made my namaste, which was always as satisfying to give as receive.

The room was dark and stiflingly hot; chinks of light from the shuttered window cast long shadows on the floor and the air smelt stale. I looked around for any hint of items that had been brought in to brighten it up, but there was nothing that I could see. The paint was peeling from the walls and the concrete floor was bare. The idea of spending days here, never mind months, left me cold.

With the help of the translator, I pieced together the patient's story. As he told it to me, he was smiling; there was not a trace of self-pity in his demeanour. Like a lot of the Nepali people, he viewed his accident as his fate and therefore something that just had to be accepted. All the time his wife busied herself folding his clothes. She did not speak except to greet me with a forced smile that didn't quite reach her eyes. Later, I began to understand why his wife was hurting, why she was angry with what had happened to them.

Many spinal units in Nepal are so woefully underfunded that they cannot provide nursing care, so family members have to stay with each of the patients. Specialised spinal units are few and far between in Nepal. As wives are expected to care for their husbands for the rest of their lives they often have to leave their children behind, never knowing when they will see them again, in order to keep their hospital places. Without a change in their circumstances, they often effectively lose their children.

As we were leaving the room, one of the doctors turned

to me. 'It is very common that the patients and their families have to make these impossible decisions. I'm sure that you can understand that life in a wheelchair is not easy here. It is very hilly, and the road surface is very uneven.'

I nodded. I had been struggling to walk here. To say that Nepal was hilly was the understatement of the century.

'And then there is the problem of jobs,' the doctor continued. 'Most of the work available is hard manual labour, which people in a wheelchair would not be able to do. There are no welfare payments for disabled people so the truth is that, in very poor rural areas, the injured can often be pushed out of the family home as they cannot afford another mouth to feed.'

'So, where do you discharge them to?'

'We try to train the family member who comes with them in physio and also about the physiological side of the injury so they can help with their rehabilitation. We hope this will help them return to their homes and that having a family member who understands their injury will help persuade the extended family that they can still have a future. In the new hospital, we hope to have the resources not only to aid their rehabilitation but to train, educate and help the patient find work. This will help not only them, but their families as well.'

'So, people won't lose their children?'

The doctor nodded. 'As you know, these injuries do not only affect the injured. The repercussions are immeasurable.'

As I mulled over what the doctor had told me, I followed him into the physio room. I tried to pay attention as he showed me their equipment. There was a TENS machine that looked as if it would have been used to start a car battery back in the Seventies, a standing frame and a tilt table that were both worn from repeated use. And that was it. That was the sum total of the rehabilitation equipment the hospital had. Three items that would have been written off thirty years ago back home. Don't get me wrong, the staff were amazing and doing everything they could with what little they had; there was no complacency here – just an utter lack of resources.

If only they could have the medical care I had back home . . .

For the rest of the day I was quiet. I couldn't take it in. It was hard enough for me to stay positive in the comparative luxury of the hospitals I had stayed in, let alone out here. Yet the patients and staff did what they could to stay sunny and bright. There was no complaining from them. They just got on and did what they could with what little they had.

It was a sobering visit and had given me a lot to think about.

With the official part of our trip over, Lois and I travelled up to the Himalayas. I couldn't make a trip to Nepal and leave without visiting some of its mountainside villages. There would be no actual mountain climbing for me but I had been reassured by our taxi driver that there would be some excellent views to soak up.

Lois and I both clung to our seats as our taxi tore up the mountainside road. Buses and trucks ploughed down towards us, honking their horns impatiently as they overtook each other on corners. I was constantly alert to the drop only a couple of feet from the tyres of our taxi that would plummet us hundreds of feet below. Seat belts didn't seem to make much of a feature here, so I gripped onto the driver's headrest and tried not to look down.

Our starting point was Nayapul, a small village that is an entry point to the Annapurna region. Hikers, climbers and kayakers milled around in clusters as our taxi drove past them to the drop-off point. Some were preparing for the adventures ahead; others were clearly returning from the wilderness. I soon found out that their state of disarray and their general aroma was a key indicator of which direction they were travelling.

Stepping out of the car, the first thing that hit me was the heat. It was overwhelming. If, like me, you had assumed the Himalayas were cold, you would only be half right. The largest mountain range on Earth is not actually that far from the equator, so the ice and snow you see is the result of altitude. Where I was, in the foothills of the mountain slopes, the temperature was above thirty degrees and very humid.

Pleased to be back on solid ground, we made our way to the Nepali man who was holding a sign with my name on it.

'I am Bigraj,' he said, shaking our hands and smiling shyly at us.

We introduced ourselves and in a few minutes we were off, this time on foot. We followed Bigraj as he led us away from the busy hut where the tourists met their guides. Soon we were on a road that doubled as a dirt track that wound its way above the green valley below. Every so often we would have to cross a precarious wooden rope bridge that hung over the water streaming below. If my leg went into spasm, I knew that I could easily be sent tumbling into the rushing water.

Trying to take my mind off whether the swinging bridge could take my weight, I decided to ask Bigraj if he had grown up around here.

'Much higher up,' he responded, as he expertly crossed the bridge in a few short strides. 'From age four or five, like many in Nepal, I had to climb stone steps to go to school. I climb for an hour each day. I will take you to stone staircases soon. The best views up high.'

'So how did you become a guide?' Lois asked from up ahead.

'When I was fourteen I work as porter, carrying the bags of tourists while guides showed the way. I was interested in the languages. I managed to learn English by talking to visitors. Nine years later, I was promoted to guide. I have been walking these mountains for nearly thirty years now, so I have much to show everyone.'

Listening to Bigraj helped calm my nerves as I made my way slowly to the other side of the bridge.

After a couple of hours of clambering up the valley, we stopped off in a little homestay/restaurant for lunch. All of these small mountain villages seem to be run by the same character, a smiling yet authoritative older woman who I shall just call Grandma. As you can imagine, all of the locals are incredibly fit with hardly an ounce of fat between them . . . well, most of them. Grandma is undoubtedly top of the food chain. Whilst the others work the fields or carry huge loads thousands of vertical metres, Grandma is in the kitchen cooking up a storm to feed them all. She may have been taking liberties with the portioning, but it seemed like a fair deal – the whole place would collapse without her. And, like all grandmas around the world, her food was always delicious.

We sat down at the side of Grandma's house and Bigraj told us the food options.

'What do you think we should order?' I asked.

'Dahl Bat,' he responded. 'You should order it at all the homestays. You will see why.'

Dahl Bat is a local dish that's a combination or rice, lentils and pickles and, if you were lucky, a bit of meat on the side. Following Bigraj's advice, Lois and I promptly ordered the Dahl Bat.

As we waited, I noticed another tourist couple wander in

who ordered one of the other dishes on the menu. Grandma rolled her eyes in response. When we had finished up our delicious Dahl Bat, Grandma bustled over and politely offered us seconds while pointedly ignoring the other couple when they had cleared their plates. There were no seconds for them as they'd gone off-piste. Bigraj was a wise man.

After we had finished refuelling, we thanked Grandma, crossed the road, and set off up a stone staircase that literally disappeared into the clouds. All of the villages up here are linked by stone staircases and beautiful ones at that. Hand-chiselled, narrow flags of stone were laid three deep to create each step. They had been produced by many hands and the amount of work that had gone into them was awe-inspiring but completely necessary – the villages had to be accessible in all seasons and because of the acute gradient, pathways would either be too steep or not wide enough.

As I began climbing each step, I realised that I might have taken on a bit more than I'd been prepared for. The uneven nature of the stone steps meant that every placement of my foot required some consideration and I was grateful to have my walking poles with me to take some of the strain.

Step by step, I worked my way up the mountainside, concentrating on each movement. One misplaced foot or pole could bring nasty consequences and, considering the isolation of the villages, it wasn't the best place to be injured. After half an hour of this, the strain began to build. I really struggle with lifting my left leg vertically, but it's much easier for me on a pathway as I can swing my leg upwards. I therefore have real issues with stairs and I hadn't realised that we were expected to climb them for the next five hours. My right side has to work twice as hard as my weaker left side so my heart rate was sitting at between 160-175bpm for five hours. To put this into context, the average person's heart rate during a marathon is 160bpm over four hours. There are large parts of these physical challenges that I hate – the pain, the frustration and the negative thoughts. But the rewards are always worth it . . . and, as we climbed higher, I knew this time was no exception.

After a few hours of strenuous sweating and soul searching, the path flattened as we neared the village where we would be staying for the night. There was still a sheer drop to my left but the village was only fifty metres away and I could almost smell the Dahl Bat. Staring up ahead, I wasn't concentrating on where I was placing my walking pole and I missed the pathway. All my weight went to rest on thin air and I tipped over the side of the mountain path.

I swivelled around and made a grab for the ledge but missed.

As I fell, all I could think was, *Oh no, not again. You absolute idiot.*

With a crash, I landed in a bush six feet below. That bush literally saved my life. If I ever return to the area, I'm going to head back up there and buy it a beer.

Lois shouted out and, in a few moments, both her and Bigraj's worried faces popped over the side of the walk-way. I lay on my back, staring up at them. Glancing down at my legs, I noticed a bamboo stick poking into my right calf. Panic flooded through me as I had no sensation there so it could have easily pierced my leg by several inches and I wouldn't have been able to feel it. Touching my calf, I was relieved to realise that the bamboo was blunt and would only cause a bruise.

Bigraj hopped over the side to help me as I wriggled my way off the bush. I couldn't help but laugh, probably in relief that I hadn't injured myself, but Lois hadn't found it so funny;

for the rest of the walk up to the village, she pointedly ignored me.

The village of Ghandruk nestled amongst the steep green peaks of the lower mountain range and it felt as though it had been there for thousands of years. The cobblestone walkways and drystone walls provided a picturesque scene. And that's before you even considered the views over the expanse of mountains that are some of the most famous in the world.

It wasn't until I hobbled onto the rooftop seating area at the teahouse where we were staying that I really took the time to look at where this hike had brought us. The size of the Himalayan peaks was overwhelming. They didn't look real – how could anything be that big? Wherever you looked, there were vast snowy peaks stretching up to the sky to meet the clouds, reminding you just how small you are in relation to the rest of the world; and, therefore, how insignificant your problems really were. It was a form of mindfulness just to look at those sights and remind yourself that you were only a small dot in a timeline you will occupy for a brief moment. The mountains were here before you and will still be there when you are gone.

As I sipped my beer and took in the view, I thought about what we had witnessed over the last week. A simple visit to a hospital had changed me and I wondered whether Lois had been affected in the same way. Neither of us spoke for a while until I gently nudged her.

'I can't stop thinking about the hospital,' Lois said. 'If we'd been born somewhere else, it could have been me who had to give up my children to care for you.'

'I know,' I responded. 'It's hard not to compare the two.'

I turned to her, the sun beginning to set to the west. 'There's got to be more we can do than just raise awareness. It doesn't seem like enough. It isn't enough.'

Lois is normally the cautious one when it comes to our future plans. She recognises that we both need to earn enough to eat and keep a roof over our heads. I think of those things last and consequently need her as a balance. I therefore braced myself for her sympathetic but practical advice.

'I agree with you,' she said. 'It isn't enough. We should be doing more. So, let's do it.'

My eyes widened as she clinked her bottle of beer against mine.

Sometimes we need people to tell us when we're on the wrong path, as my parents did with me and my brother when we became obsessed with computer games. And sometimes we need our loved ones to take the right path with us, so we can have the confidence to realise our dreams.

CHAPTER 19

ONE YEAR LATER

A year passes quickly when you are doing what you love.

Lois and I, together with our friend Olly, had taken the leap and set up a non-profit organisation, Millimetres 2 Mountains. The name had come from my own recovery experience, and our founding principles were: 'Purpose, Perseverance and Progress'. At this point, we were still waiting to get charity status, which would take about a year. In the meantime, we had wanted to start on raising funds for the spinal unit in Chitwan; all three of us were determined to see it built within the next few years. None of us was taking a wage from the company and we were running it and raising money in our spare time. Lois would work on our projects in the evenings after she finished her full-time job. Olly and I had more time to give and worked on it solidly for a year. I was still getting regular work speaking at functions and presenting for Channel 4, which helped pay my bills. Everything was starting to come together.

We started off small – a few fundraising evenings that worked really well – but my dream was to get people up mountains so they too could understand the transformative effects these experiences can have.

That's how, exactly a year later, I found myself back in Nepal. This trip would be very different to my last one as I'd brought thirteen people with me. We were all there to climb Mera Peak and raise money for the Neverest Foundation to build the new spinal unit in Chitwan.

At 6,500 metres, Mera Peak is the highest trekking mountain in Nepal. It's three times the height of Mont Buet and over six times higher than Snowdon. There is only a 50 per cent success rate for summitting and I knew the odds on me completing it, especially with my injuries, weren't great. We would be walking for fifteen days and it was by far my longest and toughest challenge.

Fortunately for me, two star physios who were now close friends – Wyn from Bath hospital and Kim from Salisbury – had agreed to come and climb with me to raise money. I was hoping that if I completely seized up then at least one of them would be able to get me moving again.

We had advertised the trip and passed on the cost price to those involved on the understanding that they would fundraise for their climbs as well. I already knew some of our band of fourteen, but there were a few new faces also. At the last minute I'd managed to persuade Rich, who was best man at my wedding, to come with us. He'd been having a rough few months and I eventually wore him down by constantly reciting the benefits of mountain climbs. He'd put his faith in me and I was determined that he would be converted.

It was the biggest of our events and I was more than a little nervous. I'm not known for my organisational skills but somehow I'd managed to get all fourteen of us over to Nepal and I'd spent hours poring over our itinerary. I hadn't wanted us to breeze through Nepal, climb a mountain and quickly exit.

You could be anywhere to do that. Instead, I'd decided that we would spend a few days in Kathmandu, then take an extended route up Mera Peak. If we simply scrabbled up and down the mountain, it would take eight to ten days; instead, I'd plotted out a thirteen-day trek that would take us through the less travelled pathways and villages so we could experience a bit of Nepal. I'd heard stories that Base Camp at Everest was a bit like a motorway for tourists and I didn't want our trip to be like that.

Stepping outside the arrivals lounge, I was enthusiastically greeted by Bigraj. I'd asked that he be our head guide, and he'd helped plot every day out to the tiniest detail. After several namastes and handshakes I introduced him to our group. I hadn't seen him since I was last in Nepal, but we'd kept in regular contact over the months we had spent organising the next fortnight.

After a few minutes, he ushered us to the minibus and we all piled in. We were off.

Thamel is the climbing district of the city, a bustling maze of mountaineering shops, bars and guest houses. To the casual observer, the sheer volume of people might seem like chaos, but it has its own rhythm that we, as tourists, had to adopt. Nothing highlights this more than the traffic situation. Right of way is judged by who beeps first, lanes are deemed optional and pedestrians are merely obstacles to be driven around. Throw in a few motorbikes carrying entire families and their livestock and you've got one hell of an obstacle course.

Standing on the edge of the pavement and trying to judge when was best to cross gave me heart palpitations the first few times. The traffic never slows and there are no zebra or pelican crossings – the Nepali people are in continuous motion. The only thing was to step out and cross.

After a false start where I quickly turned and scuttled back to the safety of the pavement, I realised that the key to it was confidence. Put your best foot forwards (in my case, my right) and march across that road at a steady pace like you belong. All of the motorbikes, mopeds and Tuk-tuks would weave their way around me. If you stop or panic, that's when you throw the timings off and could cause a pileup of gargantuan proportions.

The next day, full of confidence because of my new road-crossing abilities, we headed off to Swayambhunath, which is also known as the Monkey Temple. It's perched high up on a hill overlooking Kathmandu and is a must-see for any visitors. As I took in the gold-leafed dome and colourful prayer flags that swept above our heads, I noticed that one of our group, Arron, a friend from Bath, was holding back. Whenever a monkey came within ten feet of him, he would twitch and hide behind Rich and me.

In the end, I had to ask what was wrong.

'I might have forgotten to get my rabies jab,' he replied, rubbing the back of his neck and eyeing up a macaque who was staring down at him from its stone perch above.

Rich and I looked at each other and raised our eyebrows.

The next two hours were spent with Arron on high alert trying to dodge the monkeys while Rich and I ushered them his way.

After some dinner in a local cafe, Bigraj stood up and gave his first rundown of what lay ahead.

'Last year, I did a little three-day walk with Mr Ed. Very easy. This year, big challenge.'

I gulped down the last of my beer. I wouldn't have described our trek last year as either 'little' or 'very easy' and I didn't think Bigraj was the sort to exaggerate either. I smiled and kept quiet as he described the temperatures we could expect on the mountain and effectively rubbished most of the kit we had brought with us.

Bigraj's final words on the matter stuck with me. 'Mera Peak very bad for frostbite. More people lose fingers and toes on Mera than any other mountain. People think it easy, don't bring right kit. Lose toe.'

We all looked at each other – it was time to go shopping. Bigraj led us through the jostling crowds, past several decent-looking mountaineering shops, and took us straight to Shona's, the best place to buy equipment in town. I was fortunate that Berghaus had given me most of my kit, so I only had to hire a -30°C sleeping bag and mittens but Shona could have sold me the whole shop.

As our group rifled through her offerings, I stood at the side as she laughed at people's water bottles – 'Ha! Are they for toilet?' – or inspected their mittens – 'You not like your fingers?'

We knew there was a sales pitch with every sentence, but her equipment knowledge was second to none. We all stumbled out of the shop having hopefully increased the odds that we would return with all twenty digits.

On our last day in Kathmandu, I took the group to the spinal injury unit outside the city, which had been completely funded by donations a few years before. This unit is the only functioning specialist rehab hospital in the country and an example of what could be achieved if we raised the funds for a replica in Chitwan. I thought it was really important that the group could see what they were climbing for. I could talk to them about it for hours but nothing would compare to seeing it with their own eyes.

The outside of the hospital wouldn't look out of place in a travel brochure. The columned entranceway gave a suitably impressive welcome and an attractive clay-tiled, covered walkway wrapped its way around the building, providing shelter from the sun and rain. It was a far cry from the dilapidated building I'd visited in Chitwan last year.

We were firstly shown around the physio rooms where I got the chance to inspect the equipment – all newly purchased and plentiful. The employment training rooms followed on from there, where desks were laid out with laptops and patients were learning new computer skills.

Next were the wards.

I've always found walking onto a spinal ward emotionally difficult. Not because it took me back to being on a ward myself but because I was witnessing some of the most difficult times of people's lives. As we walked past the rows of beds, parents looked up from caring for their children and offered up empty smiles that were difficult to receive. It's common for children in Nepal to be employed to scale fruit trees and pick the produce. There are no harnesses and few safety measures. As a consequence, the main cause of spinal injuries is falls from trees and children disproportionately suffer from them.

Walking around, I understood the patients' pain but I don't think I will ever understand that of a mother or father, wife or husband. I'd witnessed that their emotional wounds were often deeper.

To finish up, I was asked to address the older patients. After I'd spoken to them, they told me how lucky they felt and how they wanted to help others when they were discharged. Their levels of positivity were amazing.

As we left to go back to our hotel for the night, I said to

Rich, 'I told you that it's not just me who wants to help others after being injured.'

He'd been unusually quiet for the walk around the wards and I could tell that he was having to process what he had seen.

Lukla Airport has one of the most famous runways in the world, mostly because it's hanging off the edge of a mountain. As our plane circled the gateway of the Everest region, I couldn't pull my gaze from the sun rising over the Himalayas. The golden light spread across the clear horizon with only a solitary cloud keeping sentry over a particularly prominent peak – Everest.

After our plane safely landed on the most dangerous runway in the world, we headed off for breakfast. The surrounding mountains provided an impressive backdrop to the multicoloured, bustling streets of Lukla town. Trekkers, climbers and Sherpas were either picking up supplies before heading north or celebrating their return to civilisation. It was a transient place, and, soon after we filled our bellies, we passed through it as well.

The first day of trekking was six hours of stone staircases. I still found them a battle as I faced the same difficulties with my movement. However, every time I lifted my head, the rewards were more than worth it. Vast bamboo forests spread out in every direction and their soft rustle accompanied our every step. We hadn't seen many Westerners since we'd left Lukla and this is how I wanted it to be. It would take us a week to reach the bottom of Mera Peak and then the real challenge would begin. The dense forests we were walking alongside were a welcome distraction, but all too soon I had to put my head down again and climb another hundred steps.

Mid-afternoon we arrived at our teahouse, pleasantly

shattered. Our accommodation was typical of what we would expect over the coming days: several corrugated iron sheds that each slept two people. The beds were simple wooden platforms that we laid our sleeping bags on.

Sleep is obviously key when you are producing an energy output that is the equivalent of running two marathons a day, but it wasn't coming very easily. As I lay there on my first night, tucked up in my sleeping bag, I was finding it difficult to nod off. I was essentially lying on a plank of wood, so I was constantly shuffling around as various parts of me went numb from the pressure. Fortunately Rich didn't snore, but the walls were just a piece of plywood so it felt like we were all in a bed together. Every noise reverberated through the millimetre-thin walls.

When I woke up the next morning, I stepped outside and took a deep breath of cool mountain air – there is no better way to start the morning. Add a cup of masala tea and a chapati egg sandwich with chilli sauce and you've got the perfect start. The food was delicious and thankfully abundant as I was burning through more calories each day than I could replace. This was a real concern for me, as the last time I returned from Nepal I looked as if Lois had been gobbling up my rations. In preparation for this trip, I'd spent several weeks happily padding myself out by having doubles of everything. I now had some reserve fat to fuel me, which would hopefully stop my body from attacking my muscles if times got too tough.

Our morning trek took us straight into the jungle as the treeline on the mountains in Nepal doesn't end until you reach 4,000m. It was a very pleasant start to our day to weave our way around giant rhododendron bushes and across a few mountain streams. Inevitably, it wasn't long before we veered off the main path and up the side of a mountain, or hill, depending on who you're asking. Nepalis don't consider anything under 6,000m a mountain, and that's not the only thing they view differently. As I struggled up another uneven trail, Bigraj dropped back to walk beside me as one of the other guides took the lead.

'What's the rest of the route looking like?' I asked, frowning as I began to lose sight of the people up ahead.

'A little bit up. A little bit down. But mostly flat,' was his response.

Anyone who has been to the Himalayas will understand the concept of 'Nepali flat'. And let me tell you, it's never bloody flat.

After about an hour of battling my way up a stone staircase, I turned to Bigraj. 'Are you sure we're not lost? I don't remember this being on the daily itinerary . . .'

He laughed. 'A little bit up.'

Cheers, mate.

We spent the rest of the day circling the edge of a mountain/bloody big hill, yo-yoing back into valleys before climbing up to the next ridge. I'm not sure at what point we hit the Nepali flat but I must have missed it while I was taking a swig from my water bottle.

After seven hours on the trails, we arrived at the village of Panggom at 2,894m. Bigraj had told me that the views from this village were stunning, but, when we stumbled onto the grass at the edge of the village, we were met with a thick mist that hindered any possibility of mountain gazing.

After another restless night in a plywood shed, we left Panggom and found ourselves climbing a concrete staircase up to a monastery perched above the village. The mountains had now revealed themselves and, reaching the top of the steps, it was clear why this spot had been chosen as a holy site. The stone building was adorned with wooden prayer wheels and the intricately painted entranceway pulled you inside. As I entered, and my eyes adjusted, I was met with a wall of colour. Three stately, golden Buddhas took up the centre piece but what caused me to linger was that every inch of the stone walls had been painted in brightly coloured patterns. It was clearly a spiritual place, but also one of joy. To think that if I'd believed my recovery would end with just the use of my arms, I would never have got to see this place.

Reluctantly leaving the monastery, we started on a path that eventually brought us to the valley that we would be following for the next ten days up to Mera Peak. After about twenty minutes we rounded a corner and there she was; rising high above the clouds, the three tightly nestled snowy peaks of Mera stood aloft in what appeared to be another world. I stopped for a moment and stared up at her. I had been dreaming of this moment for a year and to finally see her was both daunting and inspiring. I now had something tangible to aim for.

After a good night's sleep, I stepped outside and was met by an orange glow over the mountains. I was filled with energy, but little did I know how much I was going to need it that day.

The route I had chosen was unusual, but the positives of it were that as a group we were able to experience a glimpse of Nepali life and stay away from the tourist trail. The negatives were that the further we went, the less trodden and therefore tougher the trails got.

That morning, we trekked up a path that was so narrow that it was only wide enough for one foot at a time. As I lagged farther behind the group, I started to feel frustrated that I was holding everyone up. Those narrow tracks were dangerous for me as I struggle to walk in a straight line. Thick roots snaked their way across the path, and I was constantly having to stop to figure out where best to place my foot. I fell farther behind, so I forced myself to try to catch up. For once it felt like the forests were pushing in on me, trying to hold me back. Several times I fell, crashing to the ground. I would lie there for a moment while people ran back to check on me. It was humiliating; I wanted to be at the front, not lagging behind holding everyone up. Before my accident I had been so fit and now I was a source of worry.

I crested a particularly tough ridge and faltered when I realised that the way down was a near sheer drop. I joined my friend, Arron, who was staring at the valley below.

'I think I'm going to need the harness,' I said.

He nodded. 'I'll hold on to the end. Hopefully I'll be able to stop you if you slip.'

On went the rope secured to my backpack that the Sherpas had fashioned for me. Arron took the strain and I began to pick my way down the slope, the loose gravel threatening to pull my legs from under me. The concentration required was intense and every step threatened to send me, and possibly Arron, free falling down the ridge into the valley below. If I fell, I would be responsible for risking Arron's life as well. The pressure was mounting – it wasn't just my safety at stake any more.

By lunchtime, I wanted to curl up in a ball and not get up again. Normally, I never let on when I am struggling. I'd had enough tough days in the hills and mountains to know that they would pass, but this one was different. I felt utterly defeated.

We all decided to break for lunch and I hobbled off by myself and sat on a fallen tree trunk. I was usually in the centre of things but I needed some time alone.

I had started to question myself; could I go on? The route that I'd picked was more treacherous than I'd ever imagined and the climbs down the mountainside pathways were bordering on dangerous. The amount of concentration required to navigate them safely meant I was holding everyone up. Our itinerary was slipping and I was the sole cause of it. We had another three days of trekking and then we'd actually have to climb the mountain. I leant my head in my hands, my curled left fist unable to straighten out and support me properly.

I squeezed my eyes closed and thought of everything I had learnt in the past two years, searching for something that could help me.

As I picked through this list, Arron walked over to me.

'Can I sit down?' he asked.

'Of course, mate,' I responded, barely lifting my head.

'Been some pretty tough trails today,' he continued. 'I think we've all been struggling.'

I nodded, trying to form the words to tell him that I was thinking about leaving them and retracing my steps. One of the guides would have to come with me . . .

'I'm holding everyone back,' I said, unable to meet his eye. 'If it carries on like this, I don't think I'll make it.' I paused for a moment. 'I've never said that to anyone before.'

'As far as I can see,' Arron said, kicking the dirt with his boot, 'it's all a mental challenge from here on.'

I looked up at him.

Arron stood and held out his hand. 'We've got this far. So, we've got to convince ourselves that we can keep going.'

CHAPTER 20

LUCKY

So, with the help of the group, I carried on.

What followed was the toughest day I'd had since I was discharged from hospital. The pathways we'd been following disappeared until we were traversing rocky inclines that only a local would know were there. After climbing for an hour, the trail would twist and plunge downwards and any progress we'd made felt like it was unravelling.

Bigraj was a superstar as always, leading the way while regularly checking on the rest of us.

'How are you?' he asked, after zipping back to the end of the line to see me. The strain in his voice was clear and he kept on glancing up at the sky where the afternoon sun was progressing overhead.

'I'm fine. More importantly, how are you?' I asked, pulling my left leg up a particularly high mound.

'Fine, fine. We all be fine.'

Back he jogged to the front of the group and I looked up as he disappeared. In the time we'd known each other, I'd never once heard him come close to being stressed. 'Calm' was his middle name. To know that Bigraj was worried made me put my head down and crack on.

And he was right to be stressed.

Before long, the sun dipped below the horizon and we were plunged into darkness. Our head lamps came out. The lack of natural light made the way even more treacherous and it wasn't just me at risk of falling now; we all were. The jungle was eerie at night – unfamiliar animal calls made my spine tingle as the nocturnal creatures began their hunt for food.

The temperature plunged as I scrabbled up a grassy hillock on my hands and knees, the only way I could think to get up it. Bigraj kept on flitting back and forth between us. He did all he could to help everyone and never once made any of us feel that we had to go faster. He knew it was his job to try to get us there safely and that was going to take time, not speed.

When we finally staggered into the grounds of our teahouse, it was so cold I could see my breath in the air. We had walked for nine hours and every single one of us had struggled at some point during the day. Together we'd picked each other up, both mentally and physically. An evening meal of Dahl Bat and Sherpa's stew was gobbled down before we headed to bed in our tin shacks. It was the toughest day I'd ever had in the mountains and I was pleased to see the back of it.

The next morning, I woke up early and found another member of our group already sitting outside. James had been very quiet at the beginning of the trip and I'd half expected to wake up one morning and find that he'd gone. But, as the days passed, he had begun to open up more. It was his dad who had contacted me and arranged for James to join us on the trek. James had been an officer in the army. He'd completed a few tours of Afghanistan and seen some harrowing sights that I couldn't even begin to imagine. He had been discharged from the army and had spent the last six years trying to get back on his feet.

'How did you sleep?' I asked, as I sat on the bench next to him.

'Really well,' he said, looking directly at me. 'For the first time in six years, I slept long enough to dream.'

His response floored me. I wondered how he'd coped all those years without proper sleep. We sat quietly together, sipping our tea from metal mugs and watching the sunrise.

It wasn't too long until the rest of the group joined us and we set off for another day of trekking. At 4,000m, our views for the day had dramatically changed when we rejoined the main trail following the banks of a river. Gone were the swathes of forests and jungle. In their place was low-level scrub and a rocky terrain bleached of colour.

After three hours we reached the village of Kotc where an afternoon of much-needed recuperation and washing commenced. We all had strict limits on the weight of our bags as the Sherpas were carrying them as they climbed ahead. This meant limited clothing and we'd all begun to smell. Up to this point we'd had no means of drying anything due to being on the move all day.

We were in luck that day as the sun was out, as was the wash trough and soap. A few of the group paid an extra 300 rupees (£2) for a warm bucket of water to pour over their heads, whilst others relied on trusty baby wipes. Either way, there was a chance that by the end of the day we wouldn't create such a collective pong.

It was not only our surroundings that had dramatically changed at the 4,000m line; the temperature had as well. That night was so cold that I kept my down jacket on inside my sleeping bag, and I could see my breath as I talked quietly to Rich. In four days' time, we would be attempting to sleep 2,000m higher in a tent, so this was still relative luxury.

The following day, we made a gradual ascent above the treeline, and it felt like a completely different world. We followed a cascading glacial river upstream towards the looming snowy peaks that seemed to have snuck up closer overnight. The path was wider and, apart from a few boulders, much easier for me to walk on than the forest trails.

It may have been easier underfoot, but we were so far above sea level that you could feel the air thinning. The idea was to slowly increase the heights we were reaching each day so that we could acclimatise, which was not something to be ignored. If you ascend a mountain like Mera too quickly, you increase your chances of altitude sickness, which is the body's reaction to a lack of oxygen at high altitude. It causes headaches, vomiting, dizziness and shortness of breath. If the symptoms are ignored, they can lead to huge complications with your heart and lungs, even death – it's certainly not something to 'struggle through'.

A couple of hours into our next day of trekking, we passed a couple of English guys who were making their way down from the peak.

As they passed, one of them said without stopping, 'It's cold up there!'

I stopped and shouted after him. 'How cold?'

He turned and gave me a big grin. 'Fucking cold!'

Suitably forewarned, we prepared ourselves for the drop in temperature that was coming our way.

As we settled down for another day in a teahouse, I reflected on my progress that day. I had finished with a completely different outlook to the day before. The new terrain suited me and I was no longer flagging at the back. I wouldn't be racing anyone to the top, but it was nice not to be the person everyone was waiting for. I felt strong, motivated and full of hope.

But mostly I was glad I hadn't given up – that's the difference a single day can make.

We spent the next couple of days acclimatising in the village of Thangnak. Every morning, Bigraj would lead us off for an acclimatisation hike where we would go higher, test our reaction to the altitude and then go back to the village. I'd begun to notice the huge difference in temperature between the sun and shade. During the day, it was quite easy to burn if you didn't put sunscreen on; but as soon as the sun dropped behind the mountains, it felt as though your nose could drop off. Wind chill also played a big factor, so our corrugated sleeping sheds actually looked quite inviting.

Two days later, we headed up to Khare village, which was around the 5,000m mark where we would spend another couple of days acclimatising.

The air was becoming noticeably thinner and sometimes it was difficult to even think straight. That's probably why I was left speechless when we rounded a giant boulder and Mera came into full view. The sky was heavy with grey cloud but every so often a sharp ray of light broke through to touch its snowy mountain peak. Before I knew it, silent tears were streaming down my face that I couldn't blame on the altitude.

We spent five hours slowly ascending to Khare, each going at our own pace as we stopped to wonder at the views we were presented with.

We were all beginning to suffer from altitude headaches but the chance of a two-day break to acclimatise kept us going. I found the best way for me to cope was to count a hundred steps and then stop to let my heart rate drop below 130bpm. It also gave me the chance to soak in the views of the soaring peaks that now surrounded us.

Now that we were starting to get back to the main trails, we had passed a few people on their return journey. Some successful and some not. Everyone who stopped to talk informed us that it was even more beautiful at the top but that summit day was particularly difficult. Bigraj was happy with the way we were progressing, but we all knew that the real challenge was yet to come.

Another thing had changed for me in the last couple of days. Because of my injuries, my hands had seized up in the cold so Rich had become my mum. First thing in the morning, I couldn't do anything for myself so he patiently helped me get dressed, zipped and buttoned me up and put my shoes on. He'd even open up my fly for me during the daytime when I'd lost all dexterity in my hands. I insisted on dealing with the rest myself when I needed to pee as I thought that might be crossing the line of friendship.

Our evening at a teahouse in base camp was a much livelier affair than I'd anticipated. It was a melting pot of different nationalities with teams either on their way up or back down again. Stories of success and failure reverberated around the dining room as Italian and Russian groups compared notes. Listening in, I found out that high camp had nearly blown away the previous day, a couple of people had returned badly frostbitten and had to be helicoptered out, whilst another group summited successfully and had returned to the teahouse triumphant.

I suppose the message was that you have to respect Mother Nature. She was largely in control of whether you summited or not.

The next day, we made our way from base camp and began the seven-hour climb to high camp. Smatterings of snow began to appear underfoot and, as we pressed on, the temperature dropped far into the minus figures. Sunglasses were essential even at these temperatures as the glare off the snow was blinding. Mid-afternoon, one of the group had to turn around due to exhaustion, so we were down to thirteen. As we climbed higher, the relatively smooth surfaces of the compacted snow suited me – it was like walking on tarmac and I was able to pick up my pace.

That afternoon we inspected our two-man tents on a rocky outcrop that was clear of snow. Rich and I sat at the edge of our tent. We were above the cloud line where the grey jagged rock contrasted with the white of the snow line. Below us were plump clouds nestling around the mountains. It felt like we were sitting with the gods.

'I wish Tom could see this,' Rich said, hugging himself.

I turned to him. 'He would've loved it.'

I'd been thinking about Tom a lot recently, what he'd missed out on and how much I missed him. I'd never got over his death, just through it. He was the one who had always pushed me forwards and I had done the same for him. In my lowest moments I had always thought of him and how he would have told me keep going, that everything was there for me to take, if I just dared to try for it.

'He'd still say you were playing a risky game by coming up here,' I said to Rich, raising an eyebrow.

'Nah,' he responded. 'He'd know someone would have to help you get your boots on in the morning.'

I grinned at him. 'Come on, let's find out what's going on with the food. We'll need all the energy we can get for summit day tomorrow.'

The temperature dropped to minus twenty as we clasped

our bowls of Sherpa stew and watched the sunlight touch the peaks of Everest and five of the highest mountains in the world. Before long, the last of the orange flames slipped away and left us in darkness.

At 5,800m, we were so high that the oxygen levels had dropped to almost half of what they would be at sea level. On the way up, you account for this by breathing harder or walking slower. But when you sleep, your body falls into its normal breathing pattern and as a result you wake gasping for air every thirty minutes.

We bunked down at about 7 p.m. as we knew that we had an early start for summit day. Every half an hour or so, one of us would gasp for air and often wake the other one up. It was like being back in hospital in Bristol with the blood pressure alarm going off all the time.

At 9 p.m. we heard a commotion in the tent behind us. The guides were talking loudly amongst themselves and we could hear someone retching. The fittest member of our group had succumbed to altitude sickness and had to be taken back to base camp by one of the guides. It was becoming more and more obvious that we were at the mercy of Mother Nature and I began to think, *What the hell am I doing?*

I'd probably snuck a couple of hours sleep when a rustle outside of our tent let us know it was time to get up. It was 2 a.m. but with a rush of adrenaline I was wide awake.

Rich sat bolt upright next to me. 'But it was my cheese grater!'

'What?' I said, turning to him.

'Ah, nothing,' he said, looking around him. 'I was dreaming that someone nicked my chee— oh, it doesn't matter.'

He scrabbled around in the dark for our head lamps and

fitted mine over my forehead. Switching it on, I could see that the interior of our tent was completely covered in frost. It glistened in the light of the torch like spider webs in the morning dew.

Rich helped me dress, my clawed hands curled up and refusing to perform even the simplest of tasks. Fortunately, they were perfectly positioned to grip my walking poles, which I, and everyone else, would need that day. I was hoping a bit of life would come back to my hands once the sun came up.

Next on were our harnesses. We would be crossing glaciers that morning so we all had to be harnessed and roped to each other. We weren't actually secured to the mountain as the idea was that if one of us slipped and fell down one of the many crevasses, our combined weight would stop them from falling any further. Part of me wondered if this theory depended on who fell first . . . surely Arron would just pull everyone down with him.

With little light pollution, the night sky was alive with stars watching over us. The head lamps were essential for picking out detail, but the moonlight illuminated our way so that I could at least see the peaks in the distance. As we began our journey upwards, my hands and feet began to burn from the cold and I was starting to get frostbite in my big toe. It penetrated deep inside me and threatened to make my body seize up. I had never felt cold like it and dealt with it in the only way I could – I retreated inside of myself where there were no thoughts. Just one foot in front of the other. I'd only managed this before when I was in hospital and wanted to try to cut myself off from what I was facing. To be able to access this place of respite again was comforting.

After about an hour we stopped, and I looked up to

see a congregation of headlamps. Two more of our team had to turn around due to altitude sickness and one of the guides led them away. I could barely mumble, 'Get down safe', before they were gone. We were down to ten.

I was now walking behind James. One of the best things about the trip was meeting him. He'd really opened up in the last few days and was now the life and soul of the group. I'd already decided I was going to award him the 'Golden Crampon', which is the award I would give on each of these climbs to the person who had contributed the most and got the most out of the trek. To see his transformation was a real joy and one I wouldn't forget.

I put my head down and zoned out for another few hours. One foot in front of the other. I ignored the biting cold, the wind attempting to freeze the skin on my face, the aches in my left side as it refused to wake up and the headache I was developing from the altitude. I ignored all those discomforts and pains and just concentrated on the current minute, the current second, as each step brought me closer to my goal.

I was jolted out of my trance by the red hue over Everest to the east. The sun was rising. As I became more alert to my surroundings, the doubts began to surface. With every step my body screamed at me to stop, but I knew things about myself now. I knew that my mind almost always gave up before my body and therefore I still had some gas in the tank. I had too many reasons to be here, too many reasons to want to succeed. And I was going to draw on all of my strength to make it happen.

Dipping my head, I pulled myself away from the tantalising views and stared down at my feet again and the snow underneath them. I needed to leave my body again and the thoughts that were trying to make me stop and turn around . . .

A shout from up ahead made me glance upwards. One of the group was pointing to the summit, which was only a few hundred metres away. For the first time I looked around and took in where I was. The world's highest mountain, Everest, had a magnetic draw and I wondered if I would ever reach its summit and stare over at Mera. It felt like I was standing at the junction between the sky and the Earth. It was at that moment that I knew we would make it to the top. With the summit in sight we couldn't turn back now.

With the last few steps, the cold seemed to recede and the sky brightened. A year of planning and dreams culminated in this moment. I was the first quadriplegic to summit Mera Peak and I'd achieved something I'd never thought possible, even when I'd been able-bodied.

As the sun hit my face, I closed my eyes. In my mind, I traced my steps backwards, down Mera and on to the plane. Further I went . . . back in time. On to the peak of Snowdon, where I realised what I wanted from life. Time wound back, to a key in the door, my wheelchair at the bottom of the staircase – discharged from hospital, independence having been fought for. In a split second, I was back to Salisbury Hospital, taking those first tentative steps, Lois always by my side. Weaving my way in the ambulance, I found myself in Bath and standing for the first time, Pete showing me that anything was possible. Travelling through the lanes to Bristol, a twitching toe, a spark of life in my finger. My family holding vigil, watching and waiting. Back to the operating theatre where Mr Barua made an incision and saved my life. Into a speeding ambulance where my heart stopped three times and my story nearly ended. To the side of a pool where I watched my younger self humming to himself as he kicked off his shoes, about to dive in.

Would I stop him? Would I tell him not to take those next steps?

No.

I wouldn't change any of it. Without that ten-second incident, my life would not be as it is now. I had been thrown a curveball and I was playing it. Through my accident, I had found purpose, and that is what everyone needs to lead a fulfilled life; not riches, power, an able body or an exceptional mind.

Purpose is what fulfils us and often we have to embrace change to find it. I had learnt that from all the people who had come before me and successfully played their own curveballs. No matter what difficulties they had faced, the ones who could genuinely say they were happy were the ones who had found purpose and meaning to their lives. I knew now that I'd never really had this before my accident. But the perspective I had gained from nearly losing everything, and the satisfaction I got from helping others, had led me to accept and even embrace my injuries and their outcome.

I hoped that others would take courage from my story and apply it to their own lives. I had learnt that the human mind is incredibly adaptable. With the right mindset, it doesn't take long to accept the past and start looking forward to the future.

Someone called my name and I blinked, opening my eyes. The wind picked up and whipped around the peak of Mera. I knew how lucky I was to have seen this, but it was time for us to climb back down again. Back to my new life – the one I wouldn't swap for the world.

ACKNOWLEDGEMENTS

I hope that this book acts as an acknowledgement to all of the amazing people who have got me to where I am today. Without the support network of brilliant healthcare professionals, trusted family, passionate friends, committed charities and inspirational strangers, I quite simply wouldn't be here, never mind sat writing the acknowledgments to my first book!

It's impossible to personally thank everyone who has impacted my life – otherwise this would read more like a telephone directory and take up an ungodly amount of space on your bookshelf – but I can't end without naming a few.

Firstly, to my mum for bringing me into the world and showing me what unconditional love is, and to my dad for teaching me that hard work and having fun can go hand in hand. To Sue, for unashamedly doing anything and everything to help, and to my brothers Josh, Chris and Harry for keeping me entertained in hospital along with all of my weird and wonderful friends. To the surgeon Mr Barua, for giving me a fighting chance, and to Pete Bishop, Wyn Lloyd, Kim Small, Ceri Parham and Restart, to name but a few, for helping me turn that chance into results. To Matt Hampson, Henry Fraser and David Smith, for providing inspiration from the start, and to all of the thousands of people who continue to do so every day. I thank you all. I know she wouldn't want it, but I must thank Bev James for persuading me my story was worth telling, and Kate Fox and Lisa Milton for agreeing with her. Also, a huge thank you to the incredible Amy Warren for holding my hand and helping me tell my story in a way that I couldn't have done on my own.

Finally, thank you to all of the whacky and wonderful people that broaden my mind on a daily basis, including of course my incredible wife and mentor, Lois, who gives me purpose in everything that I do and wilfully joins me on this beautifully unpredictable journey that we call life.

MILLIMETRES 2 MOUNTAINS
FOUNDATION

COULD YOU HELP OTHERS FACING ADVERSITY?

Initially we established the Millimetres 2 Mountains Foundation to support the spinal unit in Nepal, which we still proudly do, but the main aim of the charity has developed into offering others facing similarly difficult challenges in life the same opportunities I've been lucky enough to have. I recognise the undeniable impact that the outdoors has had on my recovery, and I want to help others experience that too.

Every year we take beneficiaries facing mental health struggles because of adversity on adventures across the globe. These trips act as a catalyst for change, after which we offer on-going support in the form of life coaching, funding towards therapy, career grants and much more to ensure the individual can take steps toward a brighter future.

I never dreamed I would be in the privileged position to pay forward some of the amazing support I've received, and we wouldn't be doing it without the generosity of so many so from the bottom of my heart . . . thank you.

To find out more about Millimetres 2 Mountains, or what you can do to support us, please visit:

www.millimetres2mountains.org

ONE PLACE. MANY STORIES

Bold, Innovative and
empowering publishing.

FOLLOW US ON:

@HQStories